THROUGH THEIR EYES

INSIDE THE MIND

Edited By Kat Cockrill

First published in Great Britain in 2020 by:

Young Writers
Remus House
Coltsfoot Drive
Peterborough
PE2 9BF
Telephone: 01733 890066
Website: www.youngwriters.co.uk

All Rights Reserved
Book Design by Ashley Janson
© Copyright Contributors 2019
Softback ISBN 978-1-83928-643-8

Printed and bound in the UK by BookPrintingUK
Website: www.bookprintinguk.com
YB0427Y

FOREWORD

Since 1991, here at Young Writers we have celebrated the awesome power of creative writing, especially in young adults, where it can serve as a vital method of expressing strong (and sometimes difficult) emotions, a conduit to develop empathy, and a safe, non-judgemental place to explore one's own place in the world. With every poem we see the effort and thought that each pupil published in this book has put into their work and by creating this anthology we hope to encourage them further with the ultimate goal of sparking a life-long love of writing.

Through Their Eyes challenged young writers to open their minds and pen bold, powerful poems from the points-of-view of any person or concept they could imagine – from celebrities and politicians to animals and inanimate objects, or even just to give us a glimpse of the world as they experience it. The result is this fierce collection of poetry that by turns questions injustice, imagines the innermost thoughts of influential figures or simply has fun.

The nature of the topic means that contentious or controversial figures may have been chosen as the narrators, and as such some poems may contain views or thoughts that, although may represent those of the person being written about, by no means reflect the opinions or feelings of either the author or us here at Young Writers.

We encourage young writers to express themselves and address subjects that matter to them, which sometimes means writing about sensitive or difficult topics. If you have been affected by any issues raised in this book, details on where to find help can be found at *www.youngwriters.co.uk/info/other/contact-lines*

CONTENTS

Belvidere School, Shrewsbury

Ellie Stennett (11)	1
Olivia Johnson (13)	2
Florence Lily Allmark (11)	4
Eleanor Parker Valero (11)	5
Lottie Williams (11)	6
Tommy Stuart Neil Clayton (11)	8
Alysha Hnatiuk (13)	9
Matilda Battrick (13)	10
Lilia Rene Ostrowski (12)	11
Tom Johnson (11)	12
Joe Raeside (12)	13
Martha Wigley (13)	14
Honour French (11)	15
Ellie Williams (11)	16
Francesca Lilly Jones (11)	17
Jasmin Ann Smith (12)	18
Jana Gemal (11)	19
Alex Budd (13)	20
Ellie-Mae Slack (13)	21
Lola Pruden (11)	22
Olivia Simpson (13)	23
Melodie Warrender (11)	24
Harrison Roberts (11)	25
Josh Thomas (13)	26
Megan Board (13)	27
Reagan-Lewis Boden (11)	28

Brighton Aldridge Community Academy, Brighton

Guluzar Aslan (12)	29
Molly Brailsford	30
Lauren Hawkins	32
Reuben Warren Cleal (12)	34

Ellie Luckhurst (12)	35
Beth Salvage (14)	36
Paige-Leigh Rowley-Pettit (15)	37
Cerys Colman	38
Rose Amy Pilcher	39
Gina Granger (12)	40
Alisha Evans (12)	41
Sonny Rosher	42
Esmé Barkaway (11)	43
Robert-Leigh Weston	44

Cleeve School, Cheltenham

Willow Bay (12)	45
Grace Stone (12)	46
William Owen David-Green (13)	48
Amber Morris (12)	50
Evie Phyliss May (13)	52
Alex Bailey (11)	54
Ruby Beaver (11)	56
Eleanor Decker (12)	58
Ellie Stipling (13)	60
Daniel Hending (11)	62
Bethany Netherton (11)	63
John Bryars (12)	64
Leilani Katie Adeline Debra Jones (11)	65
Millie Harries (11)	66
Jacob Justin Cole (12)	68
Daisy May Jones (11)	69
Asaah Afriyie (12)	70
Edward George Burton (13)	72
Isabella Corrigan (12)	74
Lauren Cheshire (13)	75
Lilly Richardson (11)	76
Amelie Brice (11)	77

Amy Jane Rawlins (11)	78
Sophie Iris Chattell (12)	79
Imy Stubbs (12)	80
Izzy Hyndman (11)	81
Caleb Hunting (11)	82
Eliza Lewandowska (11)	83
Leila Theyer-Pugh (11)	84
Harry James Williams (12)	85
Georgia Neve Caffell (12)	86
Tabitha Jenkins (12)	87
Corey Porter	88
Jake Parker (12)	89

Dukes Aldridge Academy, Haringey

Giovanni Rose-Stewart-Fraser	90
Karima Khanom (14)	92
Liyah Lewis-Robinson	93

Easthampstead Park Community School, Bracknell

Amber Jones (11)	95
Amaya White (11)	96
Charlotte Louise Marsh (11)	98
Hannah Drablow (11)	100
Kyle Adams (11)	101
Scarlett Proudlove (12)	102
Benjamin Dennis (12)	103
Jemima Persaud (11)	104
Aleni Oliphant (12)	105
Freddie Rogers (12)	106

Hillview School For Girls, Tonbridge

Maisie Kate Williams (14)	107
Amy Sawyer (14)	108
Tessa Hellsten (12)	110
Alex Phillips (15)	112
Charlotte O'Hara (14)	114

Knutsford Multi Academy Trust, Knutsford

Anabel Reeve (14)	115
Lily-Rose Dodson (14)	116
Alex Macleod (14)	118
Molly Gilbert (14)	120
Maddie Tucker (14)	122
Aidan Charlie Worth (13)	124
Faith Blackler (13)	126
Elly Leigh (14)	128
Joel George Young (11)	129
Grace Treadway (12)	130
Phoebe Jones (13)	131
Will Ackroyd (11)	132
Macy Naylor (12)	133
Maisie Austin (12)	134
Sophie Tillotson (14)	135
Ollie Hammond (11)	136
Ava Klages (11)	137
Izzy Jackson (14)	138
Lucas Reynolds (11)	139
Fiona Armstrong (11)	140
Charlie Heather (11)	141

Marsden Heights Community College, Brierfield

Mustafa Nadeem (12)	142
Ayaan Khan (13)	144
Farkhara Sajjad (13)	146
Hadiyah Noor-Ul-Hayaa (12)	147

Parkstone Grammar School, Poole

Lily Roake (14)	148
Zoya Vazir (11)	150
Abi Pope (11)	151
Hannah Palmer (12)	152
Electra Craig (12)	153
Gracie Norris (11)	154
Hermione Rose Bendall (12)	155
Freya Skelton (15)	156

St Pius X Catholic High School, Wath Upon Dearne

Shannon Burbridge (15)	157
Olivia Grace Adamson (12)	158

St Teresa's School, Effingham Hill

Evelyn Nallen (12)	159
Lucie Bryan (11)	160
Emma-Louise Norrington (13)	162
Freya Reilly (14)	164
Ruby Lebus-Smith (11)	166
Grace Howard (11)	167
Lainey Gale (13)	168

Steyning Grammar School, Storrington

Lily Bourgoin (11)	169
Isla Harvey (12)	170
Olivia Dayani Wijeunge (13)	172
Daisy Bourgoin (11)	174
Patsy Burley (12)	175
Hayden Molly Smith (11)	176

The Blyth Academy, Blyth

Summer Porter-Dodds	177
Ellie Scantlebury (13)	178
Callie Dickinson (12)	181
Aisha Anwar (14)	182
Amy Ruth Kennedy (11)	184
Holly Wight (11)	186
Eve Rowe (11)	187
Iona Thomas (11)	188
Dyllan Jon Corrie (13)	189
Ben Yarwood (12)	190
Hannah Marshall (14)	191
Cassidy Dunn (12)	192
Jean Carr (12)	193
Phillipa Eve Turner (13)	194
Bethany Welsh (11)	195
Caitlin Humble (12)	196
Ella Woods (12)	197

James Oram (11)	198
Alfie Finley McPhee (11)	199
Brooke Porter-Dodds (11)	200
Skye George	201
Kieran Hemsley (11)	202
Holly Ann Morgan (12)	203
Katelin Jane Bell (11)	204
Ayah Ghaham (12)	205

THE
POEMS

Don't Pick Me

There I was, in the darkness,
Nestled together for months as months go past,
As I grew bigger, bigger and bigger, people came to watch,
My friends were picked as samples,
There I was, all alone,
Then I was blood-red, oozing with joy,
Then I was taken.

There I was, lying amongst the other ones,
Water was splashing me (it was very cold!)
I was creasing with laughter as the water tickled me,
I fell asleep when the warm air hit me,
All of a sudden, I was poked by a wooden stick,
I was put at the front of a cart where I saw lots of people,
Someone came and gave some golden, round things,
I got picked up by the stick, wishing I was with my friends,
I could sense my friends calling me from up above,
I got drowned in oozing, brown mess.

I looked up and darkness surrounded me,
Sharp pain hit me,
I floated down a long tube
Before the time came,
I was gone forever.

Ellie Stennett (11)
Belvidere School, Shrewsbury

A Teen's Brain

When you're a teen,
Your life's a mess,
You act all mean
And you are depressed,
The mental health of a teen
Isn't great,
We put ourselves down
And we have a lot of hate.

I am a teen
Who has anxiety,
I sit between
My emotions and ability,
But I play football,
Which I really love,
I feel so small and helpless,
What on earth?

Every match,
My anxiety kicks in,
I feel so scared
And the sickness reels in,
My nerves overload
And, all of a sudden,
I just explode,

But, I take a deep breath,
Walk outside
And, in an instant,
I feel alright.

This is proof
Of how bad we can get,
For some people, it stops them
And gets in their way,
They need people to care for them,
No matter how hard it is
To keep them composed
And break through the tears,
The teens' mental state
Is not okay,
It's hard to explain,
But it's the worst kind of pain.

Olivia Johnson (13)
Belvidere School, Shrewsbury

Life In Stoneyford!

I'm a bay pony, as cute as can be,
I wake up in the beautiful paddock
With long, luscious green grass from the dawn
Waiting for me!

Waiting for John to bring me in,
Oh, what is that sound?
Creak! Creak! Creak!
The gate is opening!

John had my headcollar,
He put my headcollar on and took me to my stable,
When we got back to the yard, I was so happy,
A big, chunky hay net was waiting for me!

I chewed and chewed
And munched and munched,
People arrived, already mucking out,
People massaged and put a short cloth on my back.

Before I knew it, I was cantering,
The person on my back was very friendly,
At the end of the lesson, she patted me and said, "Good boy!"
Once the last lesson had finished, the delicious grass was waiting for me!

Florence Lily Allmark (11)
Belvidere School, Shrewsbury

Through A Phone's Eyes

This is a poem through my eyes,
Well, through my lens,
Some days are boring,
I power off and start snoring,
My owner's life is so mind-numbing,
Other phones' lives are so enduring.

One day, I was forgotten in a pocket,
When I got out, I saw a baby with a locket,
Yes! I typed,
Finally, some fun,
Even though he was very funny,
He was also quite a dummy.

The years passed by,
The baby stopped the cry,
He slowly grew up,
He started drinking from a cup.

One day, my owner got home,
He had another phone!
I was so angry,
But, then, I realised,
I was being passed down to the boy,
Oh, I was filled with joy,
He downloaded the whole lot,
Snapchat, Instagram, Scott,
I was so happy, he was still in a nappy!

Eleanor Parker Valero (11)
Belvidere School, Shrewsbury

Ronaldo

It's Saturday
And I'm going to Spain to play,
The crowd is watching,
Eager for me to score,
My son is here,
Who I really adore,
Signatures, photos and interviews,
Everyone is forming into busy queues.

It's time,
I put the captain's band around my arm,
I hold a kid's hand,
She's such a charm,
The ref picks the ball up
And everyone cheers,
The ref blows the whistle,
The men put down their beers.

They get the first kick
Because it is their home pitch,
I sprint after the wall
And I trip in a ditch.

Everyone laughs,
Humiliation, embarrassment,
It's my first game for Portugal
And I've made a fool out of myself.

I get up and run after the ball,
I just want to go home and give my mum a call.

Lottie Williams (11)
Belvidere School, Shrewsbury

Messi's Football Boot

I enter the field,
I stick in the wet turf,
My eyes are burning with enthusiasm
As the whistle blows.

I touch the ball under Messi's control,
I pass it to Suarez with elegance,
I mumble, "Let's score a good goal,
Let's block out the crowd and focus!"

I regain possession at the halfway line,
I ghost past countless defenders,
Not one, not two, but three
And win a penalty.

I line up the shot with unwanted pressure,
With my heart racing through the leather,
I step up and *boom!*
What a goal from the Argentine!

The final whistle goes, it's all over,
The game is won by Barcelona,
Messi was by far the man of the match
And I'm his boot because of that!

Tommy Stuart Neil Clayton (11)
Belvidere School, Shrewsbury

What Did I Ever Do Wrong?

F ootball days are the worst, it makes my stomach feel like it's about to burst,
O thers don't realise the pain, I, as a football, know how to get rid of the pain,
O nly footballs feel pain, not like the players who roll around in the middle of the game,
T o be honest, what did I do? I never move without being told to,
B ooting me with all their power, I don't like it, they realise I'm slowly running out of my power,
A ll alone until they return but they don't want to be my friends, they want to make my stomach churn,
L oneliness is the worst, not one person I have met has decided to let another football have a turn,
L ampard, I thought he was nice, but his kick hurt with an almighty fright.

Alysha Hnatiuk (13)
Belvidere School, Shrewsbury

My Mirror

My mirror, I hate you, deep in my heart,
I hate the way you show the truth to me,
Invading my mind, tearing me apart,
You're the reason I'm no longer carefree,
How do I hate you? Let me count the ways,
I hate your ugly face, body and smile,
Looking at you makes me cry for days and days,
But no one really thinks my hate is worthwhile,
But let me compare you to a chicken?
Nobody could ever look worse than one,
But even you look worse than a pigeon,
Why do you do these things? They can't be undone,
Why do you matter? It's all in my brain,
You're just my reflection, my image, my pain...

Matilda Battrick (13)
Belvidere School, Shrewsbury

Fear

The fear I felt,
Oh, the way she put me on the grass,
How dry and green it was,
I didn't like it,
The fear I felt.

The way he called me to eat my food,
It looked different from my mother's,
Oh, I miss my siblings,
The fear I felt.

The sky began to dim and scared me very much,
I could hear the TV in the living area,
They called me up
And I ran away,
The fear I felt.

I was in the dark, scared and fearing,
My first night was weird, worrying and scary,
I don't know why they wanted me,
I am clumsy, yet they care for me,
I feel fear no more.

Lilia Rene Ostrowski (12)
Belvidere School, Shrewsbury

The Glue Stick!

How would you like it?

Being rubbed on paper constantly
And then having a *kid* screw your lid on,
Every day, layers rubbed off your face painfully,
When your lid comes off, all you see is a grotty kid.

How would you feel?

All of the other kids rewarded with a new pen,
Looking so happy but the pen is gutted,
Children should be charged
For making us stationary miserable for life!

"Bad boy!" the teacher shouted,
"Do not wreck my pens or glue stick!"
"You are guilty," the glue said,
"You are silly," the pen said.

Tom Johnson (11)
Belvidere School, Shrewsbury

I Will Believe

L ions are cool and aren't dull, but you humans should be in zoos,
I can't believe you treat us so bad since you are mad,
O h! Why do you? My family and friends know I am the loneliest.
N obody should be doing this, please stop it!
S o, you don't listen to our peace, I guess it is war!

R ule like us since we are nearly extinct, we will be like the dodo,
U s lions and other species are not mean, you shouldn't be so mean,
L egally you should know at this rate the world will be gone,
E w! You kill just for fur, just to shave us!

Joe Raeside (12)
Belvidere School, Shrewsbury

Frozen

I stand there, frozen,
For I have just killed a man,
Animals in cages, beasts in chains, yet,
They are just men,

I lie there, frozen,
For I have just killed a man,
As the fluid drains from the needle,
The blood drains from me,
My head goes light,
My legs collapse,
The world goes black around me.

I sit there, frozen,
For I have just killed a man,
The guilt, confusion and pure terror
Hang like a smog, floating around the room,
Am I any better than them?

The cell halls are laced with dread and horror
Because I have just killed a man.

Martha Wigley (13)
Belvidere School, Shrewsbury

My Chinny Chin Chin!

So many hairs upon my chinny chin chin,
I can't ever smile, not even grin,
So many so horrible and cruel,
Yet, I never speak, I'm such a fool,
I'm always alone, can't use a phone,
Can't text my friends, just play pretend,
Everyone's so big, oh so tall,
I can't make friends, no one at all,
I sit in a corner, crying to myself,
Yet, no one is afraid to be themself,
All my hairs growing grey and long,
Dancing around like a game of ping-pong,
It's nearly the end, too much pressure,
Just need a friend, now or never!

Honour French (11)
Belvidere School, Shrewsbury

Do You Really Know Me?

Unicorn, that is what I am,
I'm not pink and glamorous,
With a glorious, brushed mane,
Well, that's what all of you think I am.

Apparently, I dance on rainbows
And eat candyfloss
And I grant wishes with my so-called horn,
Well, let me ask you,
Have you met me?

So, you may ask, what do I look like?
I'm grey and black with hairs on my back
And my big hooves don't give me powers to fly,
I smell like sawdust and my mane is tangled.

So, before you describe me again,
Do you really know who I am?

Ellie Williams (11)
Belvidere School, Shrewsbury

A Pen's Life

I was in a dark box with all my friends,
Then somebody loudly said, "Send!"
We were chucked and thrown
In the air like a drone,
Then, suddenly, a bright light came into the darkness.

I was kept within a school,
It's not very cool,
I was used all around
But was never ever put down,
I never got any rest.

Today was my worst,
When the fire bell burst,
I was thrown on the ground,
Then bounced around,
My ink exploded everywhere.

The children came back in
And I was chucked into the bin.

Francesca Lilly Jones (11)
Belvidere School, Shrewsbury

Love Is Everything

L aughter with playing
O ver and over,
V ery grateful,
E njoy every minute.

I love my family,
S o much love.

E verything means so much,
V ery trustworthy,
E njoy moments of life,
R ight way of life,
Y es, they love me,
T hey give me lots of love,
H elp me through it all,
I wouldn't have had the best start in life,
N othing can be better,
G reat compared to what could have been.

Jasmin Ann Smith (12)
Belvidere School, Shrewsbury

Poaching

P oaching is the worst way to have fun,
O ver hundreds of birds have died because of this,
A nything can kill a bird, but this is the worst way yet,
C an anyone help, help save my day?
H aving loads of birds dying, I'm afraid we'll go extinct,
I 'm a young bird, flying through the sky, and seeing birds get shot makes me sad,
N ow human friends are trying to protect us,
G oing through this is tough but can humans at least stop?

Jana Gemal (11)
Belvidere School, Shrewsbury

Soul

I see me,
Me in the flesh,
Body put to rest,
Lying in my nest.

The flames roared
As the car soared
Through the road,
The skidmark bend and the speed
Got slower.

The glass pierced through me
As I could see
Me, cold, cold like ice.

Blood shot out of me like a stream,
A stream that was red.

I can't believe it was me,
Me in that crash,
That car crash.

Alex Budd (13)
Belvidere School, Shrewsbury

Michael Phelps

Like a merman in the water,
Always supported by my daughter,
Four gold medals I have won,
Two-hundred-metre butterfly is just one.

The competition is always tough,
But never have I ever played rough.

When the whistle goes, I am off,
Anybody would call me a bluff,
Somersault off the wall
As if I were a football,
Touching the side near the crowd,
I have won, I feel proud.

Ellie-Mae Slack (13)
Belvidere School, Shrewsbury

Sit On It, Sit, Sit!

Why am I so short to the rest?
Why can't I just be the best?

People don't know how it feels,
I'd rather be on wheels,
I'm like an old book on the shelf,
It's got to be bad for my health.

I am so lonely,
There is no one to talk to,
No one cares,
I don't know how I can cope,
Oh, I do wish there is hope!

Lola Pruden (11)
Belvidere School, Shrewsbury

Mother Nature

My creations are dying,
So, people, please start trying
To put it right,
So it can go back to being bright,
It was a place for inspiration,
But now, left full of desperation,
But never forget it,
Alongside my devastation.

So, I beg you, I beg you,
Please help and all,
Love from Mother Nature,
That should be all.

Olivia Simpson (13)
Belvidere School, Shrewsbury

Power Beyond Belief

I am so beautiful, perfect and clean,
But everything isn't all that it seems,
My life is awful, all this stress,
Can't wear any clothes, not even a dress,
I hold so much power, too much, oh, I wish
I could leap into the ocean, as free as a fish!
All I want are my dreams to come true,
Don't worry freedom, I'm coming for you!

Melodie Warrender (11)
Belvidere School, Shrewsbury

Source Of Light

I am like a lamp in a bedroom,
The only source of light,
When darkness seizes the Earth
In the dead of night
With cries from a mysterious silhouette,
The wind shakes the trees
As if it were an earthquake,
The clouds are fog,
I can barely see the small villages,
When the sun emerges,
The villages fade away...

Harrison Roberts (11)
Belvidere School, Shrewsbury

Serenity

The sweet sounds and sights of serenity echoed through the forest,
The beauty of the Earth used to be honest,
Trees and vines swayed in the breeze,
All of nature lived at ease.

Trees fall and fires rage,
Controlled by people twice my age,
You murder all that you see,
You leave no future for you and me.

Josh Thomas (13)
Belvidere School, Shrewsbury

Have Some Fun!

Life gets faster every day,
No time to think, no time to play.
Hurry, chaos, lots of stress!
Tension leads to sleeplessness.

But wait, not everything's bad,
Most things are great.
So get out of the house and have some fun!
Before it's too late, when winter's begun!

Megan Board (13)
Belvidere School, Shrewsbury

All About Sports
A Haiku

Robert Firmino
A Liverpool footballer,
I'm Brazillian.

Reagan-Lewis Boden (11)
Belvidere School, Shrewsbury

Rise Up

It all started when my family fell apart,
My dad left me, my mother died,
Moved to my cousin's, he committed suicide,
A voice saying, "Alex, you have to fend for yourself."
So, I started reading every book on the shelves,
Raised enough money to go to New York,
People say, in New York, you can be a new man,
If I want to be remembered, I have to rise up.

Met new friends,
Laurens, Burr, Lafayette,
All agreeing to help our country,
The war with Britain is not good,
Not enough supplies,
We are forced to eat our horses,
I ask the general if I could lead the army,
He says no and asks me to write,
How can I rise up without a fight?

I meet Eliza, my brand-new wife,
We have a kid named Philip,
He soon dies from getting shot,
Just because he was overprotective of me,
Eliza leaves to have a holiday,
I disagree with holidays,
Ended up meeting Maria Reynolds,
Let's just say, it didn't end well.

Guluzar Aslan (12)
Brighton Aldridge Community Academy, Brighton

Through Their Eyes

They all think I'm dangerous,
Delirious,
Some people think I'm for grins,
But I'm truly serious.

When I walk down the street
Or down the market road,
They look at me,
Like *I'm* the one to beat.

To get rid of,
Obliterate,
Just because my 'lifestyle' is
Something you all hate.

I want to escape,
To run, be free,
But who can't just *leave*,
'Crazy', 'mental' me.

Caught holding hands in public,
Is that such a crime?
Just because a woman
Might love her own kind.

Brunei, my home,
Meant to bring me safety,
I plead, I pray,
"Come, now let's not be hasty!"

Drag me to the desert dunes,
Force me to my knees,
Use their fists, their feet, their words,
They make me beg and plead.

Their rocks in hand,
Horrific, sharp but clean,
Ready to be stained
By the blood of me, the fiend.

Throwing, then agony,
Blood gushing down my flesh,
The gashes, the wounds,
Even death's pain would be best.

And now, I know it's coming,
Just for being me,
Women, women loving
For LGBT.

I've had to live in secret
For what, I now believe
To waste my life,
But to have it ended by Brunei.

Molly Brailsford
Brighton Aldridge Community Academy, Brighton

Anxiety

I lie awake at night,
Curled in a ball real tight,
Terrified by the voices in my head,
Sitting alone in my bed.

You make me worry
About my loved ones day and night,
You're my worst enemy,
Hidden in disguise.

Those torturous voices in my head,
They scream to get out,
"No one likes you," is what one said,
It makes me want to scream and shout,
But I'm so tired,
Too tired to continue to fight,
I feel like my sell-by date has expired.

But I try not to let it show,
Don't want anyone to see what I've got hidden,
With shallow breath
And teary eyes,
I want to run,
I want to hide,
I need to keep it all inside.

I'm losing hope,
I'm losing faith,
I hope in Heaven I have my place.

Lauren Hawkins
Brighton Aldridge Community Academy, Brighton

Fly

Two eyes with many different perspectives,
I glance down at my pitch-black, hairy body,
My many thin legs slowly scrape across the gigantic slate of glass,
Facing the outside,
My two crimson eyes, divided,
So many views that I can hardly make sense of the beautiful world that treats me like a monster,
When, in reality, I am just doing what I have to do
To survive.
A thundering rhythm of vibrations shakes my being,
A hot, sour odour,
A shadow, raising its colossal limb,
My chitin wings begin to whir frantically,
I fly away into darkness
Gigantic collision
A sticky foundation
Wings, immobile
Bound
Trapped.
An eight-legged beast looms,
No release from the suffocating web of the spider,
It ends as it began
Darkness.

Reuben Warren Cleal (12)
Brighton Aldridge Community Academy, Brighton

Through The Eyes Of The Blind

As I get out of bed, I can hear the slightest sound,
I use almost all my senses, but one I never found,
I can hear, I can feel, I have a sense of smell,
But what dangers lurk around me, I find it hard to tell
And, although you've probably guessed,
Yes, I do confess,
I may be blind
But I still know my mind.

I still have feelings,
Although I am not the same,
I still know the game.

I don't see it as a disability,
Even though I can't see,
I can hear the quietest of things,
I can hear when someone sings.

We are no different, you and I,
But my downfall is what makes me fly,
I may be blind,
I may be odd,
But hope, I'll find
And I'm different,
Thank God.

Ellie Luckhurst (12)
Brighton Aldridge Community Academy, Brighton

Through Their Eyes

Through their eyes,
They see me,
Struggling for my life,
Around the corner, there are three.

No one around me to help,
They stand there, hypnotised,
Teachers can't hear my yelp,
Around the corner, we're disguised.

Through their eyes,
I am a popped balloon,
No air in me, just cries,
To me, they are immune.

Now, I'm in the danger zone,
Critical health, I'm ready to leave,
Desperately reaching for my phone,
Believe.

Through their eyes,
I am no more,
Flying through the skies,
Now at peace, not war.

Through their eyes,
I am gone,
You may have your allies,
But I am a phenomenon.

Beth Salvage (14)
Brighton Aldridge Community Academy, Brighton

The Mask Of His Emotions

He sits and thinks,
Through day and night
Since she left him
In a fight.

His anxiety on a high,
His mind running wild,
Finally giving in,
He smiled a crazy smile.

Lost in thought,
Lost in fear,
Forever stuck like this,
Forever stuck here.

No matter how hard he tries,
No matter what he does,
His anxiety drags him back,
Making him want to run.

Struggling to breathe,
Struggling to see,
Struggling to be heard,
Struggling to be him.

The night comes to an end,
His mask goes back on and hidden away,
Forcing his smile
He wishes would stay.

Paige-Leigh Rowley-Pettit (15)
Brighton Aldridge Community Academy, Brighton

Through Their Eyes

She works so hard day and night,
Trying to make sure everything's alright,
She thinks and worries
But doesn't let it show,
Because her face has a big glow,
She looks at me with love in her eyes,
She is my mum, the strongest woman alive,
Maybe not outside but inside
Imagine looking in my mum's eyes,
Being stressed and hard at work,
She's awake before us,
Asleep after us
And always on the go, even when she's ill,
She doesn't get a lot of time to herself,
But I know that she knows
When we get home,
Her smile glows the biggest glow.

Cerys Colman
Brighton Aldridge Community Academy, Brighton

Blind

Don't ask me how I look
Or if I can do your hair,
If you can't already tell,
I'm deeply in despair,
Now I've closed my eyes
I'll never wake up,
Oh, how I wish to use these things again,
Or even read a book,
No, I don't go to school,
Or have many friends,
Even though it seems to be,
It's not quite the end,
Through rain or shine,
Not that I can tell,
My friend will always be there,
Like a little, shining bell,
When my days are rough,
He'll always give me a hug,
My little friend called Baxter,
Baxter the wonder dog!

Rose Amy Pilcher
Brighton Aldridge Community Academy, Brighton

Feline Fun

One paw after the other,
I step excitedly out into the breeze,
A new sound, a smell and then another,
Jumping elegantly onto a nearby plant pot,
Under the shade of some trees,
I begin to chew on some leaves
When, all of a sudden, comes a big blast,
Shuddering with the new, cold chill
Something small and swift gives me a thrill,
Leaping and bounding, I go for the kill,
Slipping and sliding, I go beneath,
But, when I catch my prey, it is only a leaf,
While jumping and leaping is lots of fun,
I think it is time to curl up in the sun.

Gina Granger (12)
Brighton Aldridge Community Academy, Brighton

Through Their Eyes

Don't ask me to remember
Whether it's September or November,
I just want you by my side,
Don't be scared of me, terrified,
I still am myself, my love,
Whether I gain wings like a dove,
Don't ask me to remember,
I want to save my last moments with you,
I don't think like I used to,
Don't cry my dear,
Shed a tear,
I know the best of me is gone,
Don't ask me to remember,
Just stay by my side 'til my life is gone.

Alisha Evans (12)
Brighton Aldridge Community Academy, Brighton

Through Their Eyes

I wake up and I feel uncomfortable
Like I'm being stared at,
I wake up and turn around to see a glass wall
With people behind it,
I wake up and they bang on the glass,
Trying to get my attention,
I wake up and see in the reflection of the glass,
I'm not me,
I wake up and I have a different diet of nothing
But water and lettuce,
I wake up and I'm... a... tortoise,
I wake up from this horrible dream.

Sonny Rosher
Brighton Aldridge Community Academy, Brighton

Fire

Fire, fire, fire,
Run, run, run!
Screaming,
"Mum? Dad?"
Anyone?

My home has burnt down,
I have lost my family,
I have no more possessions,
The rainforest burnt down,
It was on fire for months.

Fire, fire, fire,
Run, run, run!
Screaming,
"Mum? Dad?"
Anyone?

The rainforest was on fire,
It was for months.

Esmé Barkaway (11)
Brighton Aldridge Community Academy, Brighton

Through Their Eyes

I am a puppy
Whose owners are always happy
And we always play,
I see the neighbour's cat
And I chase it away,
They walk me, feed me,
I sleep on the settee,
I'm just a little puppy
But I'm as happy as can be.

Robert-Leigh Weston
Brighton Aldridge Community Academy, Brighton

Have You Decided?

I'm a little brown jar with a bright yellow top,
My insides can make people's taste buds go *pop!*

I'm dark brown, I'm sticky and salty to taste,
Clean out my jar, not a drop you should waste.

On hot-buttered toast, I like to be led,
Inside a cheese sandwich, I can also be spread.

You can put me in beans or in gravy for a roast,
My flavour is unique, but I don't like to boast.

Licked off their finger, or sometimes the knife,
Some people can't live without me in their life.

My feelings get hurt when I hear people say,
"Yuck! That's disgusting, take it away!"

But when people eat me and squeal with delight,
It's then that I know that I've won the fight.

You either love me or hate me, the nation is divided,
How do you feel? Have you decided?

Willow Bay (12)
Cleeve School, Cheltenham

Perfect

"I'm not good enough!" she says,
Her long hair pinned back, so she can prod and poke,
Poke at the things that make her beautifully different,
She tries to call herself beautiful but chokes on the words every time,
I see her at the mirror, sobbing,
The tears rolling down her face as if in slow-motion,
Down her beautiful face.

The girl her family once knew was funny and caring,
She had been replaced with a distant, shy girl,
She brushes them off, telling them, "I'm fine!" and puts on a fake smile to please them,
She doesn't tell them about the boy who called her fat,
Or the girl who sends her threatening messages,
She starves herself and will not eat until she passes 'society's requirements'.

She can't tell anyone about what they've said and done,
She tries to jump from her cliff of sadness but who is there to save her from the water below,
The water, that's who,
She sinks,
Slowly sinks into depression and anxiety,
Feeling that she cannot trust anyone,
She screams for help and support, but all people see on the shore are bubbles rising,

She needs to realise,
You're never alone.

Grace Stone (12)
Cleeve School, Cheltenham

A Bully's Perspective

I don't know why
I act this way,
I guess it's 'cause I'm bad.

But when I stop
And really think,
I think it's 'cause I'm sad.

I've been told
By nearly everyone
That emotions make me weak.

That I can't cry
Or shed a tear,
Not a single whimper or squeak.

So, when my emotions
Get too much for me,
I only have one outlet.

I take it out on other guys,
Actions I know
I'll soon regret.

But what if it was okay
For me to show my weaker side?

Instead of keeping him hidden away
Through my social standard and my pride.

So, next time I feel
I will explode
And take it all out
On that boy.

I'll stop and think,
What's bugging me?
And maybe then
I'll find real joy.

Through being able
To express myself
In many different ways.

I won't explode
And bully him
And get into a craze.

So, next time
We make fun of men
For showing a softer side,

Please stop and think
What it's like
To keep all your emotions inside.

William Owen David-Green (13)
Cleeve School, Cheltenham

Why Do They Stare?

Another day of people walking by, not one person hearing my cry,
Another evening spent all alone, wishing I had a home,
They look at me with such guilt on their face,
Knowing they will return to a nice, happy place,
My entire life is here in one bag and all that covers me is a rag,
But these people don't know my story and how I ended up on these streets,
I had everything, my life was good and I even had lots of treats,
In the blink of an eye, my life changes, never to return to the same,
All I can do is hope that someone will return and help me get a job so I can earn,
I wish that I could go back to my original home, with my bed, food and a phone,
Please, someone, take me back to the time before my life turned to crime,
No one understands how lonely and sad I feel and I don't know when I had my last meal,
No one looks in my direction, the only eyes who see me are my reflection,
I'm nobody to them, just me, but I'm a brother, son and grandson to my family,
However, the shame of returning to my old stomping ground makes it hard to ask for help,

Don't just ignore me,
I don't know why you stare.

Amber Morris (12)
Cleeve School, Cheltenham

The Feelings Of The Victim

I am afraid to come to school,
Every day is a repetition of the day before,
I see them waiting for me,
Waiting to insult me, waiting to watch me cry,
Everyone just stands and watches,
They watch me, *me*, the victim of the bully
And they don't even *think* to help me,
This makes me sick.

I tell my mum and all she has to say is,
"Sticks and stones may break your bones,
But words will never hurt you!"
This means nothing to me anymore,
It's all lies,
Just lies upon lies.

I struggle to sleep at night,
Because the things they say stick in my mind,
Nobody even tries to stick up for me,
Just because they are scared that they might be next in line,
Every day, I hope and pray,
I pray that they will stop,
I pray that they will stop,
But they never do.

Why me,
Why did I have to be the victim?

Is it because I'm vulnerable?
Is it because I'm weak?
Probably.

I just wish this would all go away,
I wish it was over,
All I need is the bully to say sorry and to stop,
Is that too much to ask for?

Evie Phyliss May (13)
Cleeve School, Cheltenham

Realisation

Convinced and honoured, they travelled with me,
Dodging the reign of terror from sea to sea,
They launched us far away,
Only a monument remembers today,
Every day, blow after blow,
What struck us? We do not know.

It only ended forty-four years ago,
The rattle, the crack, the scream, the flare,
No one seems to care,
We don't know what it was like,
Simultaneously, the news delivered the worst strikes,
Where on earth did it go?
It only ended forty-four years ago.

Traumatised in the cast,
Every man did not last,
Cruelty, greed and the wants and the needs,
We prayed for mercy yet we did the deed,
The sight was like paper, challenging a knife,
It was slick, fast and took his life,
It ended only forty-four years ago.

Cents and quarters on every grave,
Their time back is what we crave,
They never knew what they were up for,
The trail of life ended in gore,

Slumped on the ground in a puddle,
We drowned in the misery rubble,
It ended only forty-four years ago.

Alex Bailey (11)
Cleeve School, Cheltenham

Leaving Home

As the days go by,
As close family members die,
Some of them survive
And will have to say goodbye.

As the bombs start dropping,
The English start copying,
The Germans fly over,
The English travel to Dover.

All of a sudden, I had to leave,
Hopefully finding a place to sleep,
Although, it was my last night,
I knew it was right.

As I woke up,
Me and my family broke up,
As I travelled to the train,
I couldn't work out what was happening in my brain.

With my belongings in a paper bag
And my little brown nametag,
The train headed south-west,
Where the countryside would be best.

I was on the train for hours,
Then met a girl called Elizabeth Bowers,
My new family were geat
And I found myself a new mate.

I knew my life would never be the same,
Would I ever see my family again?
Every night I'll pray
That I'll see them again one day.

Ruby Beaver (11)
Cleeve School, Cheltenham

Then There Were Four

It was dark for so long,
Then you showed me the world,
Fun, is what I thought,
But it wasn't the right word.

You put me in your bag
And we walked to school,
I was jumping inside,
Your books, bright and cool.

First bell went, I stayed inside,
Second and third passed like the tide,
Then fourth period, we went early,
Great, I thought, but I thought too early.

I was taken out, the lights so bright
I was blinded by the intense white
I was picked up, I felt tense
Was I really meant to be in his presence?

Bang bang, the corridor shook
Marching down the school
He busted down a door
Everyone looked

Then three people fell just like a storm
I turned and rested against something warm
"Wait, no!" I wanted to cry

Too late
Bang bang!
Then there were four.

Eleanor Decker (12)
Cleeve School, Cheltenham

The Mirror

I see tears,
I see fears,
I see empty, grey plaster,
I see only a flicker of a smile,
If only for a moment,
I see friends come and go,
Some never seen again,
Then empty, grey plaster.

I see the pressure of society,
I see the damage of truth,
I see more than just a face,
A face of beauty,
A face of regret,
I see secrets, masks,
Confidence and self-doubt,
But I always see
The empty, grey plaster.

The empty, grey plaster I see every day
Became a part of my life one day,
I see years pass,
I see time move on,
I see fear slowly fly away,
I see a spark,
A twinkle,
A modicum of hope,

The guilt has dissolved,
The pain has faded,
But the empty, grey plaster
Will always be there.

Ellie Stipling (13)
Cleeve School, Cheltenham

Hunter Gets Hunted

I am a soldier, a hard-bodied warrior,
I am the hunter of all hunters,
I don't get scared, I am the boss
But, suddenly, the plot swapped.

I was hunting my prey
As the night turned to day,
The sun rose, the sun shone,
But, I didn't realise I would soon be gone.

It was getting darker
As the plot thickened,
My prey was getting further and further,
Away from me, it seemed to be
That actually the prey was me.

I slowly turned, just in case,
To see a truck was watching my place,
I made my move, I pounced too soon,
The humans, they came,
Boom! Boom! Boom!

The dart, it stung like a bite,
I lost control, I lost my might,
My eyes were heavy, a sheet of black,
But, know this now, I will be…

Daniel Hending (11)
Cleeve School, Cheltenham

Love You, Owners

I need them, they need me,
I walk them, they feed me,
I am as happy as a child on their birthday
And they never ask for any pay,
They never fail to make me happy.

If I need them, they're there,
If something goes wrong, they care,
They always help me when I need it most,
My owners always make a good host,
Sometimes they shout at me, but it's rare.

'Man's best friend' I'm called,
Others say we're the best in the world,
Being loved is our duty,
We love you back, unconditionally,
My favourite place, up on the sofa, curled.

When you leave, I miss you so,
With you is where I want to go,
Under stiles and over walls
And through fields, chasing balls,
When you come home, my tail wags to and fro.

Bethany Netherton (11)
Cleeve School, Cheltenham

Weight Of The War

I feel the weight of the war upon my shoulders,
To win this war, we will have to move boulders,
I must do this for the people,
They cannot see me feeling so feeble.

Luftewaffes haunt my dreams,
The bombs shelters are bursting at the seams,
Screams echo in my ears,
This war has been going on for years,
Bodies lying on the floor,
I just can't stand all the gore.

Even as we speak,
I can hear the Jerry finding the targets that they seek,
But we shall not throw in the towel,
Even though their engines howl,
Like a wolf mocking its wounded prey,
They threaten to make sure we never see day,
By putting a bullet through our head
And make the last colour we see, red.

If I don't end this war,
This war will end me.

John Bryars (12)
Cleeve School, Cheltenham

Raindrop

Clouds emerge like a cage I cannot escape,
Aggressive, thundering booms pound through my ears,
A streak of electricity abruptly glimmers in my eyes,
The tears of the sky will hunt me down until I find shelter,
Pitter-patter, pitter-patter.

I keep running,
Faster and faster, not knowing where I'm going to end up,
The rain beats upon my head,
It surrounds me,
It leaves me with no choice but to get under a dry surface.
Pitter-patter, pitter-patter.

I finally find somewhere to keep shelter,
I watch the pelting liquid glow in the streetlights,
Floods of water rush down into drains,
The sweet lullaby of the rain, knocking the glass,
Makes my ears dance to the melody,
Pitter-patter, pitter-patter.

Leilani Katie Adeline Debra Jones (11)
Cleeve School, Cheltenham

Stop!

Icebergs, icebergs,
Melting away,
All because of humans
Who think it is okay,
Driving in their smoky cars,
Each and every day,
Nothing thinking about who we are,
So, here, I lay,
Alone!

I am a home to polar bears,
It's as if nobody cares,
So, here I yell to make other's aware,
Our friends find it unfair,
Their lairs
Are becoming bare,
Yelp!

My limbs sink into the sea below,
Everyone thinks that we don't know
That though this process might be slow,
Someday, we will just go,
Goodbye!

So, I know I've had the final straw,
This issue can't continue anymore,
Just think to yourself, *what are we doing this for?*

From my icy core,
I beg for it to be a law,
Stop!

Millie Harries (11)
Cleeve School, Cheltenham

Why Do They Bully Me?

Another day of people bullying me,
Why do they do it? I can't see,
They push me to the ground and steal my locker key,
Why do they bully me?

I'm lonely at break, I'm lonely at lunch,
It's only a matter of time before I get the next punch,
God, those bullies keep stealing my Monster Munch,
Why do they bully me?

I feel so angry, I've had enough of this,
If they carry on, I'll go and tell Miss,
If they would stop, it would be absolute bliss,
Why do they bully me?

I go to the teacher and tell them how unfriendly they are,
She tells them to keep their distance, stay away and far,
I see them after school when my mum picks me up in the car,
At long last, they've stopped bullying me,
God, that was bizarre!

Jacob Justin Cole (12)
Cleeve School, Cheltenham

Peer Pressure

I live down a small lane,
I suffer from mental pain,
On a daily basis, I cry myself to sleep,
As all I can do to fight the pain is weep,
I go to school, scared,
I'm never prepared.

The fear of being left out
Is what it's all about,
I don't like being rejected,
I would love to be accepted,
To get into friend groups,
I get forced to do bad things, like smoke,
They must think I'm a human joke
That they can boss around and poke.

Instead of causing myself harm,
I'm going to show my natural charm,
It's harder than you would think
For me to smile and wink,
Changing myself to fit in isn't my cup of tea,
So, instead, I'm going to be the best possible version of me.

Daisy May Jones (11)
Cleeve School, Cheltenham

They Had Everything

I couldn't breathe,
Couldn't hear,
Couldn't think,
I was hurt.

Why me?
Why me?
Why not them?
I had nothing to lose,
They had everything.

I walked over to them,
Punch,
Kick,
Jeer.

Someone yelled at me to stop,
I did it again,
Punch,
Kick,
Jeer.

All the time, I was repeating,
They had everything,
They had everything,
They had everything.

I had to go back,
I didn't want to go back,
They had everything,
I had nothing.

I was there,
But I wasn't,
They had everything,
I had nothing.

I *was* nothing...

And they had everything.

Asaah Afriyie (12)
Cleeve School, Cheltenham

War, Horrible War

We were flying over countless countries,
Flying towards doom,
Bang!
Our wing was hit,
We fell down, down, down,
Soldiers yelled, yelled, yelled.

Heart pounding, mind racing,
I jumped,
Pulling my 'chute, I landed,
A body thumped down next to me,
I panicked,
Did my brother survive?

I turned the body over,
My heart sank,
Aged only nineteen,
Three years younger than me,
He was gone,
Dead.

I grabbed his ammunition,
I dashed,
I bolted,
I ran.

I heard shots,
Bang! Bang! Bang!

I fell to the ground
And I felt blood,
It was finally over,
I was free.

Edward George Burton (13)
Cleeve School, Cheltenham

As A New Day Passes

I watch as she films for an hour a day,
I watch as she uploads a video per day,
I watch as she breaks under stress,
I watch as she breaks into a crying mess.

I wonder how it feels to be famous,
I wonder if she would rather be anonymous,
I wonder if she wants to stop,
I wonder if she's scared her followers will drop.

I sit as she watches her followers again,
I sit as she stresses, all for the fame,
I sit as she puts on a smile for the audience,
I sit as she reads hate comments full of ignorance.

I see her break down in tears,
I see her surpass all her fears,
I see her watch as others play,
I see her long for a normal day.

Isabella Corrigan (12)
Cleeve School, Cheltenham

Waste Of Life

Once I was in a notebook,
Feeling fine, yet dull,
I didn't know where I came from,
Now, the guilt is tearing me up, line by line.
I've seen my roots,
My first form,
Now, I'm looking at what I have become,
A worthless piece of waste.

I see my creator,
What I have caused,
This can't truly be happening
And I can't be the reason,
I'm just a sheet,
Look at me now,
A worthless piece of waste.

I've done such a terrible deed,
Made death from life,
For what I ask
And no response,
That's what I deserve,
I'm looking at past me
And look at me now,
A worthless piece of waste.

Lauren Cheshire (13)
Cleeve School, Cheltenham

Deer Hunting

Prancing through the trees,
Soft crunching of the leaves,
I jumped across the stream,
Agile and quick, I was nowhere to be seen.

The gunshots in the distance echoed in my ears,
As they moved closer, I remembered my fear,
I jolted around every obstacle blocking me,
I lurched myself over everything stopping me from being free.

Another two shots passed,
I heard another fall down onto the grass,
They slowly moved closer to me,
Everything around me was a blur and I couldn't see.

They stood above me, knife in hand,
Their smirk wide and grand,
I took a last breath as he pulled out a sack,
That was when it all went black.

Lilly Richardson (11)
Cleeve School, Cheltenham

What Have I Done Wrong?

One morning, I woke up to see all of the plastic
That is dumped on me,
What have I done to deserve this mess?
Please tell me, what have I done wrong?

Why treat me like trash, clearly, I'm not,
If it weren't for me, there would be no sea,
What have I done wrong?

All of the rubbish,
Plastic bottles and cans,
Why can't you see I am the sea, not a plastic rubbish bin?
Please tell me what I have done wrong?

Once upon a time, I was as happy as can be,
But now, people think I'm a piece of trash,
Why can't you just recycle?
Now, one final time,
Please tell me what I have I done wrong?

Amelie Brice (11)
Cleeve School, Cheltenham

One Little Star

Surrounded by grey,
By night, by day,
No wonder the sun doesn't come and stay,
Any spark of happiness just shrivels away,
No wonder the sun doesn't come and stay.

I'm isolated, starved and lonely,
Starved so much, I'm skinny and bony,
No wonder the wall is so high and stony,
They want to keep us trapped, enclosed and lonely,
No wonder the wall is so high and stony.

I'm in here for past, present and future,
I'm in these conditions forever
All because of one little star,
In my life, I wouldn't get very far,
All because of one little star.

Amy Jane Rawlins (11)
Cleeve School, Cheltenham

My Small Struggle

I struggle,
I'm small and sad,
I keep hundreds of feelings inside and I'm mad,
I can't take it anymore,
I'm nearly stepped on every day
And no one thinks a thing of me,
Even though I am a king in my dreams,
I carry leaves on top of me.

I struggle,
I see my mates get picked up and squished,
I just have to pray I'll be missed
If the same exact thing happens to me,
I live every day using brute force just to eat
And I wish I won't be taken by giants just for amusement,
Then, for me, I will be as happy as an ant can be!

Sophie Iris Chattell (12)
Cleeve School, Cheltenham

Pollution

The sea deep and serene,
The bright, shining moon long gone,
Sun blooming across the horizon,
Golden flakes falling into the ocean,
Gentle waves lapping against the shore,
Everything was so good before.

Plastic has changed the world,
It disrupted the environment,
With no regards for us,
I watch it as it enters my world,
The paradise marine.

All lonely and scared,
What will happen to me?
I look and I search for some company,
My friends and family, taken,
Without a kiss goodbye.

Imy Stubbs (12)
Cleeve School, Cheltenham

Save Me

Flames spread around me,
Burning and bright.
Cries of birds,
Squealing gazelles,
The hyenas laugh no more.
My own roar,
Cannot be heard,
All there is are screams and moans.
Embers fall,
Trees crash down,
Headlights burn through the smoke.
Men with guns,
Men with traps,
Caging the leopards,
Shooting elephants.
Large boots crash in my direction.
I look left,
Fire.
I look right,
Fire.
I look back,
Fire.
I look forward.
A man,
Then...
Nothing.

Izzy Hyndman (11)
Cleeve School, Cheltenham

Who Am I?

I may be a hunter
But it's clear to see,
If I have no food,
Who am I?

I may be fierce,
But when I hear the bang
Of the poacher's gun,
I run, scared, thinking,
Who am I?

I may be handsome,
But when I die
I'll lose my fur,
And, without it,
Who am I?

I used to be so happy
With family and friends,
But the poachers took them all.
And now I've heard
The bang of the gun,
And I know it is the end.

Caleb Hunting (11)
Cleeve School, Cheltenham

I Am Mother Nature!

I am the one who gives you trees
Which then you cut down!

I am the one who gives you
Majestic animals,
Which then you eat and poach!

I am the one who gave you the oceans
Which then you kill and pollute!

I am the one that created *you!*
The one that gave you this Earth!
But you keep killing me,
Thinking there will be a Plan B!

However, little do you know,
It'll kill you too!

Eliza Lewandowska (11)
Cleeve School, Cheltenham

Kicked In The Corner

I'm kicked in the corner,
All day, every day,
I try to be cheerful but no, nothing,
I'm curled in a ball, sobbing,
Facing the playground against the wall,
The sun seems delightful, colourful,
Not like me,
Just sat on the ground,
Stuck,
I want to play,
But the children don't acknowledge me,
They stand there,
Laughing,
I'm kicked in the corner,
All day, every day.

Leila Theyer-Pugh (11)
Cleeve School, Cheltenham

The Lone Crusader

Isolated on this planet,
I stumble across the desolate landscape,
Never before touched by a living man,
I stare up at the twilight sky,
"This is it, the end!" I say,
My mission to secure the star
Turned ugly,
I stare at the mangled wreck of my ship,
The rain slashing my cheeks,
I think of the humans on Earth,
Will they destroy this celestial sphere of rock
Like they destroyed theirs?

Harry James Williams (12)
Cleeve School, Cheltenham

Forgotten Friend

Here he is again, my forgotten friend!
He walks in with a smile on his face,
Strutting about as if he owns the place,
I don't know who he is but he seems quite nice,
Always bringing me flowers of a high price,
He always smiles like a friend
Even when I remind him I don't know him again and again,
Then he says it, he calls me 'mum',
That's when I remember that he's my son!

Georgia Neve Caffell (12)
Cleeve School, Cheltenham

Pollution

P lastic around my neck, I swim and dread,
O h, this will be my deathbed,
L ungfuls of plastic and polluted water,
L et's stop this slaughter,
U gly beasts humans are,
T o them, this isn't dire,
I 'm almost there,
O h no! I'm running out of air,
N ever again will I see this ocean again, today I die to the hands of men.

Tabitha Jenkins (12)
Cleeve School, Cheltenham

Bullet

As more days go by,
More animals die,
When I was in that gun,
I felt animals' hearts thump,
They go outside to the forest
And they roam around the landscape
And aim and fire, then die,
More and more die,
Until I stop myself,
Then they load me up
And I fly, until they die,
Someday, they will be left alone
And we will have no meat to live with.

Corey Porter
Cleeve School, Cheltenham

Social Media

It's what's slaying a generation,
Young folk can't resist the temptation,
Puny fingers can't avert their attention
And the elderly like myself are in great contention,
With the media that's harming the intellect of the nation.

Jake Parker (12)
Cleeve School, Cheltenham

Evil Eye

Neglected. Everything is a blur,
Tangled shapes and distorted colours,
Desperate squints and prickly stings.
It hurts.

It's not fair.
What are those objects that move, I wonder?
The unfamiliar scent of my mother's face along with my brother's?
Is the ocean's surface really a mirror?
Are those bangs and flashes really just thunder?
I wonder.

Permanently cursed.

I can't recover.

With a laser, maybe it would all be clear,
Will I be able to notice those distinct features?
Watch the rain drizzle or the stars twinkle?
Will I be able to identify the shrivelling skin when you're a soul-sucked vessel?
Witness you struggle when you're old and brittle?
Will I be able to...
Stare at our home as it's burning and wailing?
Identify our weeping trees as our land is drying?
Observe our hollow-cheeked babies crying?

Glance at all of our empty plates and the echoes of our mothers sighing?
Will I be able to look at our bloodbath, our families dying?

What if I spot a rash on your chest, a lump in your breasts?
Would I see the dark hole in your heart, the centre of your stress?
Those scars invading your body like an uninvited guest.
What if your smile's illusion is revealed to be a frown and that your entity is a mess?

I think I like the bewildering blurs, unnatural shapes and misunderstood colours.

Permanently blessed.

There's no need to recover.

Giovanni Rose-Stewart-Fraser
Dukes Aldridge Academy, Haringey

The Darkness

Blood cascaded down the portrait of sin,
Painting a morbid figure,
For creatures with caliginous skin,
Gifted with the ability to manoeuvre,
The forest of enchanted serendipity
That is a wolf in sheep's clothing.
A wonderful world of duplicity,
Devoured by the essence of loathing
Donated by the darkness.

Do you see or are you blinded like them?
Is your mind unable to comprehend the diabolical
Or are your lips sealed by a thread?
By the fear that clouds your heart
The sweet sonorous sound engraved into your soul
Whispering sweet nothings about the darkness.

Their hunger is insatiable,
For they are the offsprings of Typhon,
Coated with the agony of our ancestors
Gifted with the ability to manoeuvre
Past our deepest, saddest and wildest secrets
While we crawl back to our hiding; the darkness.

Do you hear my words or are you untouched by them?
Is your mind accepting of the diabolical?
Because you consider this your salvation,
For our sins are cromulent in the darkness.

Karima Khanom (14)
Dukes Aldridge Academy, Haringey

End

A drought becomes a sudden flood
On second, you're fine
The next, you're sunk
Trying so hard to keep afloat
Don't let them see
Don't rock the boat

Try to hold your breath
Don't blink
They know a lot more than you think

They're watching now
Stay still
Too late

They know you're weak
So they spread hate

Spread it like a foreign disease
Through words that do anything but please
Pretend that you don't hear a thing
Look at the floor
Fake a grin

You know what they say isn't true
But tell me
Who are you saying it to?
Is it for you?
Or is it for them?

At the end of the day
There is no end.

Liyah Lewis-Robinson
Dukes Aldridge Academy, Haringey

Help...

Trapped...
Within myself
My mind a cosmos, empty and silent
But one river within it...
Flowing rapidly with thoughts.
It tells me the truth and tells me the lies
My anxiety cannot be cured just by calming and breathing,
My depression cannot be cured just by smiling and relieving,
My anorexia nervosa cannot but cured by taking just another bite
And my mental illness cannot be cured...
Help.
Trapped.
In my mind.
My PMDD cannot just be cured by having operations or having therapy.
My bipolar disorder cannot be cured just by talking to someone...
I'm going crazy, lost in my mind's abyss,
Holes forming beneath me as I plummet into darkness...

Amber Jones (11)
Easthampstead Park Community School, Bracknell

Behind The Scene

As you switch off the telly
Do you ever think
What's life like behind the scene?
Do you imagine a luxurious life?
A life where I am happy
A life where I am proud
If you think that
Then you are wrong
So wrong, so very wrong
Do you ever realise
That my smile might be fake?
That's right
Almost all of what you see of me is fake
My laugh is fake
My face is fake
My life is fake
So much insecurity engulfs my body
Taking over my head
Taking over my money
So much spent
I need to sleep
The director yells
Five more minutes
Why does no one notice me?
It's like my pain is invisible
I suffer in silence

But I can't
I can't express my feelings
My feelings that I feel so deep down
My feelings I don't know how to let out
I'm trapped
I'm stuck
I'm lost
Suddenly, the director yells
"Action!"

Here I am again
Here I am again
I say this every time I go on set
But only in my head
Not out loud
Because this is my life now
Not real, fake
I can't change it now
This is me
I
Am
Fake.

Amaya White (11)
Easthampstead Park Community School, Bracknell

'Reality' TV

Three...
Last-minute make-up fixers dash across set
Two...
I glance at the script one last time
One...
We prepare to start the show
"Action!"
Suddenly, I am perfect
A vision of grace and elegance
The clumsy, kind, real version of me is locked away
A mask of fake emotion covers my face
But I feel nothing

Scripted arguments and conversations
Fake friendships and love
Words put into my mouth by drama-hungry directors
Tears fill my eyes
But I feel nothing

Trapped and oppressed by the character I have created
Forced to hide the real me
My untrue emotions and words fuel the audiences
But I still feel nothing

"Cut!"
Finally, it is over
I take a deep breath

Once again, I can show the real, authentic me
I have no clue why they call this 'reality' TV.

Charlotte Louise Marsh (11)
Easthampstead Park Community School, Bracknell

The Insanity

It's coming again,
It's controlling me.
Every move I make.
Everything I do,
It controls me.
My every move,
It's become me.
It's changed my life
It's changed my every move.
It's within me
It is me.
It has locked me in my own mind,
Like a bird in a cage, begging for freedom.
No one will know what happened.
They won't know who they are looking at,
Me or the insanity.
I want to let it all out,
I can't,
It won't let me.
I used to be normal, blending into the background.
But now, it is worse,
I'm forgotten...

Hannah Drablow (11)
Easthampstead Park Community School, Bracknell

Alone

I can feel all the laughter,
I can't take it anymore,
All that sweat around my collar
Makes me feel like I'm in the war,

It's like I'm not there,
They're all hanging with each other,
This is so unfair,
They're all friends with one another.

They all bully me,
How long is thing gonna go on?
I'm walking around nervously,
Trying to listen to my favourite song.

Why are they doing this?
I just want it to stop,
They say what's going on is no one's biz
I just want to run and ring a cop...

Kyle Adams (11)
Easthampstead Park Community School, Bracknell

My Uncle

Sweat, blood and tears
He had no fears
Even though he suffered
With his many demons
For many, many years.

Sweat, blood and tears.
He had no fears.

He loved me unconditionally.
He was always there for me,
But his demons followed closely,
They wouldn't set him free.

Sweat, blood and tears.
He had no fears

Alone that day, he ended
The pain, he had no fear alone
In the rain, our fears came true
And our tears still flow
Like a waterfall of pain
But our love will always remain.

Scarlett Proudlove (12)
Easthampstead Park Community School, Bracknell

Influencer

The fans, I can't control them
The wrong things, they take it too far
They cannot be controlled

People are attacked for harmless jokes
Crossfire caught our innocent folk
They can't be controlled

Some use it as a power
With power, bad things happening every hour
They can't be controlled

It is a power many abuse
Fans so dumbfounded, they cannot refuse
They cannot be controlled.

Benjamin Dennis (12)
Easthampstead Park Community School, Bracknell

They Are Real

An electric blanket
All cosy and warm
Secure, strong windows
When there is a storm

Big, strong harness
To lift up high
A wonderful treasure
You don't have to buy

A massive display
Of lights and illusion
A pure understanding
With no confusion

These are not things
This is how I feel
This is my family
And they are real.

Jemima Persaud (11)
Easthampstead Park Community School, Bracknell

My Cousin

My cousin was the best person I had ever met,
But life goes on.
Oh, all the laughs we had.

You are so intelligent,
Joyful and happy.
I wish I could be like that.
Oh, all the laughs we had.

He was an inspiration to me.
He never gave up.
He always stuck up for me and said
To stick up for myself.
Oh, all the laughs we had.

Aleni Oliphant (12)
Easthampstead Park Community School, Bracknell

John Cena

He's better than the rest
And he's beaten the rest
He has some obscure house rules
And he didn't show up for WWE Crown Jewel
He broke up with his fiancée, Nikki Bella
But his acting needs to get better
He's really the best
And he's full of hustle, loyalty and respect.

Freddie Rogers (12)
Easthampstead Park Community School, Bracknell

My Fury

My fury
I drum down to the ground like red ants,
Bouncing with every drop.
I am in prodigious agony,
I bellow as I hit the rigid ground,
I roar like a fierce lion as I turn grey and black,
As I fall, people run from me, screaming.
Why are they screaming?
I flash like fire,
With my electric light plummeting jaggedly to the screaming earth.
The bright lights which once polluted the luminous sky fall silent,
The inordinate screaming halts,
As my fury dissipates,
I part like a grand curtain,
To allow my old friend to penetrate through,
To restore light to the beating earth,
My fury which once filled the sky,
Evaporates like steam
And I am silent once more.

Maisie Kate Williams (14)
Hillview School For Girls, Tonbridge

A Year Of The Great Bell

I see everything,
I hear everything,
I watch everything,
Yet I'm still stuck here,
Bellowing every quarter of the hour,
So the whole city can hear me,
Can hear my roaring, ringing and raging voice,
Creating the London atmosphere,

I am 160 years old,
I have witnessed my Earth's life,
I have felt it when winter turns to spring,
The cold air rushing against my body,
Falling snow on top of my head,
My hands becoming solid, stiff,
It's the peaceful day,
Where no one is rushing for once,

Until the booming, sizzling and crackling lights,
And the big countdown starts to happen,
I suddenly let out a big boisterous yawn,
The sky above me lights up in the dark,
Everything is beautiful and sparkly,

Below me, my people cheer,
I hear the powerful beats that they play,
It's almost as if they are challenging me,

Challenging their greatest speaker,
Big Ben, that's me.

Amy Sawyer (14)
Hillview School For Girls, Tonbridge

Mother Of All

I am the Earth,
the mother of all
and I want to know
what will *you* do
when I fall?

My tears are
running out,
my lakes are
infested
by *your* filth.

What will *you* do?
Without
my gushing rivers,
my fertile land,
my luscious greenery,
my little grains
of sand.

Where will you get
your wood,
your metal
to light
your kettle?

And I need
you

to help
me *now*
by cleaning the
waters,
reusing
plastic
to help me feel,
once again,
fantastic.

Just remember,
I am the Spider Grandmother
and my web might snap.
So, before it gets
too tight,
help me
fight!

Tessa Hellsten (12)
Hillview School For Girls, Tonbridge

Stolen By War

I've been waiting,
Sitting here, watching a blank wall,
Gathering dust
But longing for their return.

I've seen too much,
Things I cannot forget.
We were charging,
Flying, across muddy,
Uneven ground
Then?
Then we weren't.

The shots
Took them from me,
My rider?
Dead,
My horse?
Dead,
Destruction is the way of man.

Only I remain
My leather,
Cracked and neglected.
Horse and rider are long gone,
Forgotten.

But us bridles?
We still remember
The ghost of our horses
Stolen by war.

Alex Phillips (15)
Hillview School For Girls, Tonbridge

Attack Of The Demon Turkey: Through The Eyes Of The Turkey

As I'm walking around the garden,
I see three young girls,
They approach me,
Why do they approach me?
Are they going to attack me?

I flap my wings in fear,
They're still near,
I keep flapping my wings so they give me room,
When one starts hitting me with a broom,
Why won't they leave me alone?
They follow me like a drone.

Finally, I can't take it anymore,
I raise my wings,
I jump off the floor,
They run inside screaming,
Victory is gleaming.

Charlotte O'Hara (14)
Hillview School For Girls, Tonbridge

Marmite

You either love me or hate me, you know who I am,
No, not Margaret Thatcher, a spread like jam.

I am very controversial so what do you think?
So is my packaging worth it or a waste of ink?

So, now you've decided if you really like me or not,
Begin this poem from the view of a Marmite pot.

So, let's begin with a simple spread,
Covering the basis of what is said.

Although I sound light-hearted and quite relaxed,
Trust me, this is sincere and contains true facts.

I find in my family, in my house, my home,
Only some people use me, leaving me so quite alone.

So, although you might not really care,
Show some respect and, in your case, share.

Share me around to those people who like,
Like me forever and spread me with delight.

Anabel Reeve (14)
Knutsford Multi Academy Trust, Knutsford

If You Need Me, I'll Be Over Here

We were laying down our lives from the start,
But we didn't know how cutting the lonely nights could be,
Or how heavy our feet would sound on the wooden floors,
We didn't know we were designed for more than creating new ways to pass the time,
No, we're only practising for that,
We're only fighting for our rights,
We're only making out new patterns, fitting ourselves with never-ending hopes and dreams,
But those fell limp and we didn't realise
There was anything else,
I didn't realise these shards of memories were left in my lungs
From the first time I learnt to crash and burn,
The fall left bruises printed up and down my arms,
Under my ribs, but I thought that was a brilliant thing,
I thought
We're supposed to fight for what we love,
We're supposed to feel the pain but
We are only a billion lonely strangers,
Laying down our lives here, I'm hoping
You'll pick up mine before it gets trampled on again,
Although we really do make the finest doormats for heavier feet than ours,
Maybe we'll remain in the dust and sand until we're burned,
But I want to be someone,
Our throats are filled so we can't ask who's gone,

We carry today where there will be no tomorrow,
So, come and lie to me,
Tell me that this all goes away,
I'm tired of playing alone in the shadows,
I need fresher dreams,
Bigger things than childhood fantasies,
They tell me I am only a lonely star,
I am only pretending, they don't see the nightmares I chase,
The graves I dig just to survive, just to bury the rot of older skins
I shed on a daily,
I lay my heart in felt-lined boxes,
Hoping it will be safer there than in my chest,
Our chests might cave in tomorrow,
Compressed by the weight of the world,
If you need me, I'll be here,
Figuring out how cold the nights could be,
I'll be laying my life down over here.

Lily-Rose Dodson (14)
Knutsford Multi Academy Trust, Knutsford

The Chair

Everyone dies, it's the one thing that's fair
And my most attractive tool is the electric chair.

If you die in the chair, then know it's your fault,
You'll see my face as you're fried by two-thousand volts.

Killers and spies, I've collected them all,
Dropped their souls into hell and watched as they fall.

Some of them protest, say execution is wrong,
They'll see quite the opposite before very long.

"All life is sacred and to kill is a sin,"
Without death, fighting crime is a war you can't win.

When you die, in the chair, you'll fall to the sulphur,
The hell hounds will greet you and there you will suffer.

You'll be burned, flayed, boiled and beaten,
The worst get dismembered, crushed by stone and eaten.

In my eternal task, I should never take pleasure,
But when I see the chair and condemn a monster forever

It ignites me with the greatest pride,
I have, at last, avenged those whom by his hand died.

On death row, they wait to walk the green mile,
Even I am disturbed by their sick, twisted smiles.

These beasts in men's clothes deserve no remorse,
If I had my way, they'd get much worse.

In my years of existence, men have feared me,
Whether I'm Anubis, Thanatos or the Shinigami.

When they sit in the chair and draw their last breath,
They look at my face and stare into the eyes of Death.

Alex Macleod (14)
Knutsford Multi Academy Trust, Knutsford

The Voice In My Head

One day, the voice creeps into your head
And slowly gets louder,
In one ear, you hear, *eat!*
But, in the other ear, you hear
That girl who tells you to eat just wants you to get bigger,
What's the point of eating if you're not going to purge?
Just do it.

Look at that photo, could you be any bigger,
"You look fine," really means, "Look at those thunder thighs!"
You're just getting fatter and fatter,
Just go to the gym.

You don't say you can have lunch,
I do or the scales do,
He's right, you're a pig,
That's too many calories,
Don't do it.

Ha, look at all of them sitting and eating lunch
While you're wandering the halls, burning calories,
Why eat that when you could be exercising?
Well done, you've lost eight pounds,
But you're still fat, fat, fat!

Once you think it's all over, the voice comes back,
Why did you eat that?

You're so fat,
That's too many calories,
Don't eat that,
Don't do it,
Just go to the gym,
I'm sick of hearing, "Just eat," as a solution when I'm not in control.

Molly Gilbert (14)
Knutsford Multi Academy Trust, Knutsford

I Am My Own Strength

No one notices the pain in your laugh,
Or the sadness in your smile,
You keep telling yourself it's only for a little while,
But, being trapped in a consuming hole for what feels like years,
Nobody cares to notice you fighting back tears,
Nobody cares to ask, "How have you been lately?"
Not wanting to be a burden, all you can do is smile politely,
It's always better to tell a lie than face the truth,
From an outsider looking in, it's abstruse,
How can someone understand
What took you years to comprehend?
But, learning the hard way, silence is an act of violence,
Speaking up and out is an act of defiance,
In this generation of civilisation,
It can't beat you down, not without your authorisation,
Never be ashamed of your pain,
It will only slowly forge a flame,
In that fire will burn a strength,
That even you, yourself will not know its extent,
It's the unspoken society truth,
Many things will happen that will break you in two,
Over time, you will be able to stand tall and say
Yes, I broke down, but I rebuilt myself trying to get to this place,

I am my own strength that you could never take away,
If you want to help in any way,
Ask a friend if they're doing okay?
We all have battles that we fight in silence,
Asking a simple question, you learn their true defiance.

Maddie Tucker (14)
Knutsford Multi Academy Trust, Knutsford

The One-Winged Fly

Born and raised, poor and young,
Feeding on nothing but animal dung,
Freezing to death in my tiny gutter,
Watching the humans eat bread and butter.

Over the weeks, getting ever more tempted,
The pure desire never-ended
For their evening meal, they had a glass of wine,
Wow! It looked divine.

So, one day, I tried to sneak through the window,
Scurrying along the pane, trying to tiptoe,
I jumped off the windowsill, buzzing around,
Trying desperately not to make a sound.

As I got through the crack of the door,
I noticed something I hadn't seen before,
It was long and thin, like a biscuit tin
And, as I got closer, I could see it was vibrating.

This 'thing' started to really intrigue me,
As I flew over the food and tea,
I got closer and closer to this fancy piece of tech,
Not realising it was a nasty threat.

And, before I could even go back to the orange juice tang,
I was suddenly hit with a massive *bang!*
When I woke up, I couldn't remember a thing,
But, all I knew is that I only had one wing.

My life will quickly end as a very little fly,
As, very soon, I will suddenly die,
Instead of being a very full guy,
I will be remembered as the one-winged fly.

Aidan Charlie Worth (13)
Knutsford Multi Academy Trust, Knutsford

The Android Sent By Cyberlife

Just a new piece of plastic,
Fresh out of the box,
Made to slowly solve,
Interrogate and influence the drastic,
Software instability at twenty percent.

I don't need a new partner!
It's not my place to say,
I have to follow you around either way,
Software instability at forty percent.

Robots that feel emotion,
What an odd sight to see,
Stopping them is what I'm made for,
Should they be free?
Software instability at sixty percent.

We can help you be free,
Should I be feeling what I feel?
Eighty percent.

Fight against the programme,
Grind it under my heel.
One hundred percent.

You're the best, partner,
That's what we've been wanting all along,

Isn't it ironic,
What I was fighting against,
I am now fighting for?

Faith Blackler (13)
Knutsford Multi Academy Trust, Knutsford

Mirror, Mirror On The Wall

The lights flickered on,
She leapt out of bed and dashed straight towards me,
As she glanced at me, her smile faded away and she let out a long sigh.

Brushes and make-up painted her face,
Wipes erased it away,
She painted herself again,
She erased it again.

She stared into my eyes, hopelessly,
Scrolling through her socials, wishing she was like everybody she came across,
The despair in her eyes grew as she longed to be *normal*.

She gazed into me,
Finally, with the *perfect* look,
She didn't really like the way she looked but knew she would fit in.

As she wandered out of her room, my heart sunk,
There was nothing I could do to help her,
I was making her dismal more every day,
Every day for the rest of her life.

Elly Leigh (14)
Knutsford Multi Academy Trust, Knutsford

Behind Bars

Why did I do that crime?
Murdered people and stole some dimes,
I was a bad man all those years ago,
My self-esteem was so low,
The name's Charles Manson,
I killed loads of people with a knife and a gun,
Now I'm behind bars,
Outside there are loads of police cars,
I really do regret it,
Now my life is pathetic,
I've been here for twenty-four years
Because I disobeyed the law,
I'm in here for forty more,
You get punched and kicked in here,
In my eyes, there are tears,
I sleep on a rock-hard bed,
It would be better to be dead,
No warmth, no privacy,
I've forgotten the feeling of being happy,
You would probably think I'm scary,
I'm not, please help me.

Joel George Young (11)
Knutsford Multi Academy Trust, Knutsford

The Bunny

Here I am in a large room
Just waiting for a loving owner,
I kept my hopes up by believing that
My chance would come eventually,
My new owners, cuddly and kind,
Would soon realise that this bunny would be theirs
And, so, from that day, my life was bliss,
Waking every morning, being greeted by a kiss,
But, after that, I saw some scary sights,
I saw violence, threats and shouting,
I heard swears and bribes
And, after all that, one human left,
I had less attention than usual,
The children felt sad and alone,
One day, I hopped away,
Never to be seen again,
I am alone, for life,
I am homeless, for life.

Every pet deserves somebody special.

Grace Treadway (12)
Knutsford Multi Academy Trust, Knutsford

Not What You Think

Who are we?
Are we merely what others see?
What others think we are?
You can't see most of what I am,
On the surface, you can only see ten percent,
The other ninety for only select to see,
I am cold
But bold,
I float in the midst of nothing,
I wish to grow
But people are making me shrink,
Sometimes, I'm the house to helpful things,
Other times for dangers,
One day in the future
I may be gone,
I will melt away into nothing
If the present continues,
They stop me,
They end me,
It is humankind's fault,
'The ice cracks',
I am the Dark Web.

Phoebe Jones (13)
Knutsford Multi Academy Trust, Knutsford

F1 Car

Here I am, at the start of it all,
Standing still and waiting for more,
The day struck when someone came,
I hoped to be looked at in fame,
But, it turns out, that the man that came in
Was actually poor,
I looked at the man and felt my pain.

I waited a day and another person came,
I hoped to be sat in and loved,
He looked at me and gave me a wave,
I thought to myself,
This is the day!
He walked towards me and he sat in me
And he said,
"Yes, this is it!"
And he hugged me!
He drove out of the dealership
And drove away.

Will Ackroyd (11)
Knutsford Multi Academy Trust, Knutsford

Through A Plastic Bottle's Eyes

I'm dropping through the sky
Like a dizzy skydiver,
I land on the mount,
Rushing down the river,
I get bottled at the source,
So they say,
Wrapped in plastic,
Two dents on the side,
Stacked on the shelves,
Here, I wait for my fate,
Bought by a mum of three kids,
Stayed in her car, it got hot,
Plucked up by Eleanor,
Then dropped on the floor,
Rolled into a drain,
Washed out to sea,
Now I'm in the Great Pacific Garbage Patch,
Floating away miserably,
It's not fun here,
But I hope help
Will be here soon.

Macy Naylor (12)
Knutsford Multi Academy Trust, Knutsford

Climate Change

My life is all in a muddle,
As I am soon to be a puddle,
I will soon be alone
As I tumble down, away from my home.

Here I am, a floating iceberg,
I see something, from the lurk,
It is a great blue whale, coming for a rest,
It does not bother me, it is not a pest.

As I float a little longer,
I get weaker but feel stronger,
What is that on my tummy?
It bits me and thinks I'm yummy.

Now I'm only half my size,
I will soon be saying my goodbyes,
Please do not start ignoring
For this is the work of global warming.

Maisie Austin (12)
Knutsford Multi Academy Trust, Knutsford

Tree Of Life

When my pages become full
And the colours shift
And I embrace the sobering brisk,
When the time has come
And my season is gone,
I have only one wish,
For my roots to remain strong
And for my life to remain long,
To survive winter's kiss.

But, fear not,
Your memories will not be forgotten,
They will remain a part of me,
They define the mark of me,
When the rain begins to pour
And you shut your door,
You might forget the sight of me,
But you will remember the might of me.

Sophie Tillotson (14)
Knutsford Multi Academy Trust, Knutsford

Turtle Struggles

There I lie, on the seabed,
Resting my trash-covered head,
My life was good, all and well,
Until I met man-made hell,
The ocean's big but too small
Until this rubbish will kill us all,
Just warned about global warming,
It's nothing to laugh about
Because dozens of species are going to die out,
Watch out! Here comes straw,
Which is lethal to us all,
Plastic bags get shoved down our throats,
Then we get hit by a boat,
Our flippers get cut,
If we would, we would yelp,
We desperately need help!

Ollie Hammond (11)
Knutsford Multi Academy Trust, Knutsford

Our Silence

Imagine the world in the future
If you kept driving that petrol car,
For there are other species on the planet,
Humans have taken this too far!

Imagine the world in the future,
If you kept throwing litter in the sea,
There are other species on the planet,
Please take some notice of me.

Imagine the world in the future,
If you kept up this horrible violence,
The other species on the planet
Would like to break free from our silence!

Ava Klages (11)
Knutsford Multi Academy Trust, Knutsford

Plastic Fish

I'm used to carry the food you eat,
What am I?
You carelessly throw me onto the street,
What am I?
By wind, I travel to the deep blue,
What am I?
A whale swims past me without a clue,
What am I?
I become entangled in an innocent fish,
What am I?
I soon become a turtle's next dish,
What am I?
A lifeless carcass washes up on the shore
Amidst marine life and plastic begins a war,
What have I done?

Izzy Jackson (14)
Knutsford Multi Academy Trust, Knutsford

Turtles

Here I am on the seabed,
Resting my trash-covered head,
Before, everything was good and well,
But now us turtles are in man-made hell,
The ocean is big but too small,
As plastic pollution will kill us all,
Each day, more rubbish is thrown away
And human beings think it is okay,
Climate change is no joke,
Plastic straws make us choke,
If you see plastic on the sand,
Pick it up, lend me a hand!

Lucas Reynolds (11)
Knutsford Multi Academy Trust, Knutsford

Puppy Eyes

When I first laid eyes on her,
Her hazel brown hair was blowing swiftly,
Her huge brown eyes stared at me gracefully,
She pointed at me and said, "That's the one!"
She picked me up and took me to her car,
On the way, she was cuddling me like she loved me,
I was getting my belly tickled and my fur scrubbed,
We arrived at my new home
Where I will stay forever with my owner.

Fiona Armstrong (11)
Knutsford Multi Academy Trust, Knutsford

The Sun's Perspective

It was alright,
The Earth, you know,
Back when there was
A peaceful flow,
Now there's just
A lot of plastic,
Making the Earth change,
It's quite drastic,
So, Earthlings, please,
Sort out your mess,
Before you all
Have to face death.

Charlie Heather (11)
Knutsford Multi Academy Trust, Knutsford

Thoughts On My Mind

Wake up in the morning, suicidal thoughts on my mind,
Mom asks what's wrong but I just say I'm fine,
A cold shiver runs down my spine
As I walk past the school gates, I know my fate awaits,
Too scared to snitch, I don't even have any mates
And, there he stands, Mr Bully, my worst nightmare,
A glimpse of him and I'm already scared,
I can't breathe properly, where is all the air?
When I walk past the bullies, all they do is stare,
Making fun of my hair, what I wear and all I feel is despair
And no one ever seems to care
And, just as I walk out the classroom door, I get thrown on the floor,
A turret of punches come towards my way and this is the cruel game that I have to play along with every single day,
There is no changing it, there isn't a way,
Suddenly, the skies turn grey and I drop on my knees and pray to God that one day
This misery will go away,
I look at my hands, all I see is red,
I can't keep living like this, I'd rather be dead,
I know Dad keeps a pistol under his bed,
So I take it and put it to my head,
Because of these bullies, I don't want to be fed,
I don't want no cheese, I don't want no bread,
My self-esteem has been shredded,

All this blood has been shed,
All these rumours have been spread,
Because of these monsters, I've been misled,
Now it's time to put this pain to an end,
All these broken feelings I cannot comprehend or amend,
I let off two shots,
Boom! Boom!
At the same time, my mum walks into the room
And it feels like being in a pit of gloom.

Mustafa Nadeem (12)
Marsden Heights Community College, Brierfield

When I Went Go-Karting

I remember the time when I first went karting,
The doors opened, cars departing.

I remember getting booked in,
When does it start? I want to begin.

I remember the marshall showing us how to drive,
How long left? Only five.

I remember the glossy black helmet and dark gloves,
Into the kart, the marshall shoves.

I remember being overwhelmed by the monster before me,
Off we go, one, two, three.

I remember the matte-black seat
And the chrome, metallic pedals beneath my feet.

I remember sitting, very excited,
Listening to the engine where fuel ignited.

I remember the dirty, grey tarmac
And the sharp corners on the winding track.

I remember seeing from the kart, fluorescent glows,
I became an angel, the wheels were halos.

I remember hearing only one thing, *vroom!*
Suddenly, it changed into a *boom!*

I remember the engine, cutting out,
I heard the marshalls begin to shout.

I remember going home soon after,
What a great day, full of laughter.

Ayaan Khan (13)
Marsden Heights Community College, Brierfield

Hope

Hope is the person you want to know,
Hope is the place you want to go,
Hope is the feeling that carries you through,
Hope is the future for me and you.

Take a moment once in a while,
Pause to breathe, reflect and smile,
I saw balloons float by,
Saw them sail into the sky,
I assumed that those who lost them
Would have tears in their eyes
But I found them, they were smiling
And were keen to let me know
That those balloons were full of trouble,
So they'd simply let them go.

Thank you, for reaching deep into me,
Find all I can be, before I can see it myself,
You never gave up on me,
I have a future because of you,
Thank you for motivating me.
Thank you.

Farkhara Sajjad (13)
Marsden Heights Community College, Brierfield

Autumn Is Here!

Autumn leaves
Red, gold and brown
Falling and swirling
Drifting down

Prickly conkers
Cracking and popping
Branches snap
Acorns dropping

Picking pumpkins
Juicy apples too
Gathering blackberries
In hedgerows for all

Foggy mornings
Damp, cold and grey
Nature's blanket
Clouding the day

Shorter days
Frosty and wet
Winter's round the corner
But not quite yet!

Hadiyah Noor-Ul-Hayaa (12)
Marsden Heights Community College, Brierfield

Dear USA

Dear USA,

Do you remember the Battle of Yorktown in 1781?
The blood and the mud and the shouts and the screams, the terror as you won?

Although it took a while and you had nothing to lose,
You were given the freedom you worked so hard to choose.

Our forces surrendered and retreated and we wished you farewell,
How would you do on your own? Only time would tell.

King George III lost America but we cut him some slack,
We said, "See you in a hundred years when you're begging to come back!"

You did well for a while, though your founders were problematic,
You managed on your own without being all dramatic.

Later on, we fought with Germany and you sort of fought by our side,
But, after the revolution, you seemed keen to run away and hide.

Three new centuries have turned over since we were joined together,
The twentieth one was miserable, as was the weather,

You seemed to be doing great, equality for all,
But pride comes before the fall.

In one terrible year, your economy was in shambles,
It was way too much for you to handle.

Wow, we thought your debt was bad back in '81,
We thought it was over but it had only just begun.

So, now, you've elected a dangerous man,
A transphobic racist with no plan.

Two hundred and thirty-eight years on,
Your pride has crashed and burnt and gone.

You've unravelled years of progress and now you're stuck,
But don't come running back to us.

It's like we predicted all those years ago,
We'll drink our tea and say, "I told you so!"

Yours,
UK.

Lily Roake (14)
Parkstone Grammar School, Poole

All You Are Inside Is Ice

How does it feel to cry without the tears falling,
Your face a mask of stone,
Pretending you're not alone?
How does it feel losing a piece of your heart every day,
Starting to crumble into nothing, like dead leaves of May?

How does it feel to look strong,
Force yourself where you don't belong?
How does it feel to come back here,
Listen to our once upon a song?

How does it feel, gazing at the stars,
Seeing nothing but their twinkling eyes?
How does it feel to be embraced in this feigned warmth,
But all you are inside is ice?

How does it feel waking up from a lie
Which you thought was your forever truth,
How does it feel getting caught
Partaking in that forbidden fruit?

How does it feel to be you,
Tell me, I don't have a clue.
How does it feel to be looking
In a mirror and all I see is you?

Zoya Vazir (11)
Parkstone Grammar School, Poole

The End Of Life

One by one, names were called,
Families wept as their loved oned
Were prised from their clasp,
I know it was soon,
When I hadn't a clue.

More names were called and more tears shed,
Then there was a pause
And then what I had dreaded had become reality,
My name was called.

Off I was marched, away from the crowd,
Then I was led far down, underground,
Not knowing what they would do next.

I was forced into a room with twenty other people,
Then a Nazi walked in and started shouting,
My German wasn't the best but
I did what the rest were doing,
I slipped off my clothes and put them in a bin.

Next we were all ordered into a chamber,
Once we were all in, I heard the door lock,
Not soon after, a blue powder rained down on us,
Encasing us in its powder

And just like that,
Darkness...

Abi Pope (11)
Parkstone Grammar School, Poole

CR7

Boots clacking against the floor,
Dreaming of that final score,
I brush my hair back out of my eyes,
As the shoelaces lie, still untied,
"Ronaldo! Ronaldo!" I heard the crowd say,
I remembered why I play every day.

I smiled as I backed up away from the ball,
I spotted a corner away from the wall,
The defenders looked at me, their eyes full of fear,
As I took my run-up, the space was clear,
I heard a whistle, clear and loud,
As silence washed over the anticipating crowd.

My foot hit the ball, sending it high,
Burying itself in the net, it was no longer a tie,
The audience cheered as the opposition fell in despair,
I did my celebration, brushing back my hair,
Bale ran up and gave me a hug,
I pictured my children jumping up,
Eva, Cristiano, Mateo, them all,
I could picture them, watching me play football!

Hannah Palmer (12)
Parkstone Grammar School, Poole

Murder In My Mind

They told me to do it,
Consequently, they threw me in this melancholy place,
I am trapped,
Slovenly walls tightened around me and visions of death sprouted in my broken mind,
I could taste the end.

I've been here, I've been there,
All within these four bare stone walls,
Whispers in my ears even though
I have been alone all these years,
Hallucinations taunt me as they morph into my fragmented reality,
All I want is my humanity, they possessed me
And won't release me from their grasp.

They don't exist but still are within my mind,
Sorrowfully planting my head in my feculent, burly hands,
I cried.

Electra Craig (12)
Parkstone Grammar School, Poole

Tears Of Sorrow

Me and the troop
Trudge to war,
Always ready
But our feet are sore.

As we march,
We all shiver,
We were fearful
As the moment drew nearer.

Big bangs
From little guns,
So, I ducked,
Thinking of loved ones.

Then, *crash!*
Men drop to the floor,
You have to expect that
When you go to war.

One by one,
The men all die,
I'm the only one left,
The end is nigh.

Then I get my gun,
Locked and loaded,
I position it perfectly,
Bang! The enemy's camp exploded...

Gracie Norris (11)
Parkstone Grammar School, Poole

The Humanoids

They wander the streets,
Long limbs swinging,
Small, cruel eyes dancing,
Clothed in fitted cloth.

What is going on in their minds?
What creatures are they that they have created this mess of a planet?
Fixated on themselves,
Unaware of their habitat crumbling around them.

But are they?
Can they save their world?
Do enough people care?
Are they blind to change?

Do enough of these weak, small creatures have the courage
And compassion to burst their own bubbles and open up their eyes?
Or will we have to do it for them?

Hermione Rose Bendall (12)
Parkstone Grammar School, Poole

Until She Drowns

She cries until she drowns,
Ignorance, yet happiness,
They don't care,
She doesn't understand,
"I never did anything!"
But is that the problem?
She's crying out, desperate,
How could you do this?
Words so cruel, does no one
Think before they storm?
Vultures screeching, picking at nothing
But a scrap of meat,
Bruises, scratches, claw marks,
Her tears flooding, never stopping,
Though she still has tears to cry.
So, she cries
And cries
And cries
Until she drowns.

Freya Skelton (15)
Parkstone Grammar School, Poole

It

He thrusts his fists against the post and still insists he sees the ghost,
He th... thrusts his fists... I cannot continue,
Memories flood back of Pennywise and his attacks.

The guilt of Georgie twenty-seven years on still haunts me
And now I see my Beverley or she was,
After the kiss she shared with me.

But twenty-seven years have gone by,
We have all changed,
Still the fear burns inside,
While ever Pennywise roams free,
The guilt and pain lives inside me
I could not save Georgie nor could I save the others,
Stanley is dead and the fear runs wild,
It spreads like fire and the memories flood back from when I was a child.

The promise was made,
The blood was shed,
This is the end -
It's time to kill the clown
Before we all end up dead.

Shannon Burbridge (15)
St Pius X Catholic High School, Wath Upon Dearne

My Rosa Parks

I was sitting there peacefully,
When the bus stopped and a white man came
And shouted at me to get off.

I was so confused, I didn't know what to do
So I waited a minute and stayed where I sat.

A crowd started chanting ugly bruising abuse
Still, I sat on the bus
And the bell on the bus started pinging.
It was then I started to get scared and my mind was stinging
No matter how loud they shouted I remained sitting.

I was terrified
Then they kicked me off,
All because I am black and I sat on the bus.

Olivia Grace Adamson (12)
St Pius X Catholic High School, Wath Upon Dearne

My Mind Is A Dungeon

Forsaken
Condemned to wander in Hell;
To suffer from my own darkness.

Trapped, cornered, cut off,
Like a kidnapper wrapping themselves around me.
My barriers are built from betrayal
And knives in my back.

Brick by brick,
Piece by piece,
I created these walls.
And now I cannot undo that damage;
Not on my own.

The lock to the door is on the other side.
The knife in the back I cannot reach.
The wound in my heart is too deep.
Only the strongest devotion can save me from this world I built.

"Love," they say, "comes from the heart,"
But I think I need a new heart;
Because mine won't work anymore...

Evelyn Nallen (12)
St Teresa's School, Effingham Hill

Timber

I am Kimkatcha of the Yanomani tribe,
son of the chief,
grandson of the founder.
My den used to be the largest,
made of sturdy wood and vines
with a comfortable bed
of leaves and moss,
now derelict from the falling Awara,
the old tree of shelter.

The beasts came at dawn,
at the rise of the majestic ball of light
over the towering canopy of the rainforest.
I was the one who heard the beasts roar
as they wiped out our beautiful home,
the adults ran clutching babies to their chests,
children trailed behind screaming,
tears running down their flustered faces,
the men in the trees collecting the fruit
were scrambling down the swaying trees,
jumping from branch to branch,
fruit falling from their clutches,
as they fought through the plantation,
to safety.

My tribe has moved eight times this year,
from shelter to an extinct mess,
at nightfall, I clamber up the great Awara
and watch as the laster sliver of sunlight
illuminates the coral sky,
so I can see for miles.
So far, in fact, I can see the next attack approaching.

Lucie Bryan (11)
St Teresa's School, Effingham Hill

You And Your Sunrise Smile

Swirling darkness,
Hair-raising tension,
The darkness enveloped me,
I could feel the apprehension,
Chills creep up my spine,
Sitting in the room,
My emptiness enfolds,
I am encased with gloom.

Then suddenly,
Like a sunrise,
Your smile lights up the Earth,
I faintly snuff my cries,
I yearn for you,
I need you,
I wish for you,
I crave you.

You take your hand in mine,
I let the feeling linger,
You're what I desire,
I only bite my finger.

You notice this, however,
And I am ashamed,
Then I turn scarlet,
My face is inflamed.

You are my voice.
The unsung hero of the tale.
But you leave me behind,
To follow your trail.

You're like a sunrise,
I'm like the dusk,
We are so different,
But it is you I trust.
You and your sunrise smile...

Emma-Louise Norrington (13)
St Teresa's School, Effingham Hill

Candourfloss

One day I will die
Leaving no lasting mark
And honestly?
I can't wait.

I amount to nothing
Especially next to the heroes
And honestly?
I would anyway.

The only pathway that cuts a groove
Is the path of villainy
And honestly?
That is worse.

Besides, I like our heroes
It's just that they make me feel small
And honestly?
Is it just me?

But I always feel sorry
For those teams of kids
And honestly?
Don't you too?

I do think it's a little cool
That we can feel sympathy, pity, for so many

And honestly?
It is really.

There's a song lyric that says that better
There always is
And honestly?
I should care.

Freya Reilly (14)
St Teresa's School, Effingham Hill

Little Brother

My little brother hides the TV remote.
My little brother chases the goat.
My little brother screams out loud,
He's scored a goal but it's disallowed.
My little brother falls down with a thud,
He likes to roll around in the mud
And he thinks he's funny
When he's covered in honey.
My brother is a pain
And dances in the rain
But at the end of the day, he's my little brother and that's okay.

Ruby Lebus-Smith (11)
St Teresa's School, Effingham Hill

Sorry: Apologies From A Bully

Sorry for kicking the bins around,
For making my room a mess.

Sorry for throwing a chair in class
And scribbling on the desk.

Sorry for punching the boy on the nose
And kicking him in the shins.

Sorry, I really am.

Sorry that I forgot my homework
I guess that's detention then
Oh well, I've had lots.

Grace Howard (11)
St Teresa's School, Effingham Hill

Ghost In The Light

The tendrils of my hair illuminate beneath the amber glow.
Bathing.
It must be this one.
The last remaining streetlight to have withstood the test of time.
The last yet to be replaced by the sickening hue of the blue-green of the future.
I bathe. Calm; breathing air of the present but living in the past.
The light flickers.
I flicker back.

Lainey Gale (13)
St Teresa's School, Effingham Hill

That Artificial Christmas Tree

When people rejoice, I am there
They gather round me and gaze
When people sing, I am there
They reach up at my peak and stare

When people dance, I am there
My branches reaching out to them
When people receive, I am there
My base the cove of treasures

When people give, I am there
I watch from my corner in awe
When people sleep, I am there
I examine the plate left on the table

When people wake, I am there
As people jump in glee
When people leave, I am there
Wishing them well on their travels in silence

But then I go, I have to
They stretch out to me one last time
And then I'm gone
I'm back in that tatty box in the corner of the attic
Just 365 days to wait
364, 363, 362...

Lily Bourgoin (11)
Steyning Grammar School, Storrington

The Mechanical Wolf

I started with the heart,
Small, fragile, breakable,
Yet that needed to change,
It needed to be strong, powerful, fearless,
Every piece was crucial.

I studied the wolf for days,
It took weeks, months
And then that glorious day came,
I had all the pieces to the puzzle,
I just needed to put them together.

The brain was next,
Intelligent, yet somewhat stubborn,
I flipped through my notebook,
Ink smudged, sentences crossed out,
But it was there, the answer.

Months had passed,
Daytime to night-time,
A wolf came to watch sometimes,
Cautiously spectating,
As I built its mechanical self.

At last, it was finished,
A masterpiece, my proudest moment,

I flicked the on switch,
Both wolves stood up
And walked out the door.

Three years ago, that was,
I've waited for their return,
Who knows where they've gone?
I don't, that's for sure,
But I wait, as the cogs in my heart turn endlessly.

Isla Harvey (12)
Steyning Grammar School, Storrington

Carrie Hope Fletcher

It was the end of the day,
Les Mis was finished,
The end of crowds applauding
As I take my final bow
Tears are prickling in my eyes,
This can't be the end.

Shan squeezes my hand,
She knows how I feel,
I walk backstage,
I see the crew I'll never see again
Where did the time go?
This can't be the end.

I delicately remove my Fantine costume,
But it's practically gone.
I was no longer Fantine,
As I grab my bags I think,
This can't be the end.

Packed bags on the subway,
Looking through show photos,
This is my stop.

I walk through the door,
Drop my bags
And straight to bed.

That's when I realise
This *is* the end.

Olivia Dayani Wijeunge (13)
Steyning Grammar School, Storrington

The Learning Pit

I am the learning pit
And at least once in your life, you will probably get stuck,
When you're doing a maths equation or your art homework,
You will probably fall into the depths of me,

Like when you're first learning that algebra sequence,
Or learning how to draw eyelashes,
Because I am the learning pit,
The learning pit is me.

When you fall into me,
You will be learning,
Learning how to get out,
Because some people enjoy being in the learning pit,
It's called the joy of not knowing.

So when you get stuck in me and it will happen again,
It's better to fall into me then jump over,
Because I am the learning pit,
The learning pit is me.

Daisy Bourgoin (11)
Steyning Grammar School, Storrington

Justice

You say those things you aren't supposed to say,
You call me what you please,
You call yourself the king of this place,
And us? All your fleas.

You dig yourself a deeper grave with each waking day,
You don't realise that words hurt
And all you do is smirk - don't smirk
Until you wash self-love away.

You take that power - that unfair power
And use it as you like,
But then you come back around
And when we're not looking you strike.

Are you out for blood?
Are you upset? Did something make you this way?
You seem like a nice person at surface,
But it seems you've gone astray.

Patsy Burley (12)
Steyning Grammar School, Storrington

Greta Thunberg: Save Our Earth

Earth is being trashed
Its oceans turning into a toxic soup
Earth is being destroyed
Its forests are getting chopped down
Earth is losing its animals
Turtles, elephants and more are being hunted

Mankind is releasing fossil fuels
Into the air
Try to reduce the amount you use your car.

Mankind is littering
Each time you drop your rubbish
Think of the poor animals you're killing.

Mankind needs to make a change
And Earth needs to be saved.

Hayden Molly Smith (11)
Steyning Grammar School, Storrington

True Love

If roses have petals and butterflies have wings
If the birds sing and sing
If you have a voice of gold
Then I have a heart of gold
You and I have the same tender soul
You and I are the goal

When the lake evaporates and the leaves change
Our love still stands
Through the night and the day
Even though we are apart
Our love is together forever and ever

If I am the peas and you are the pod
Then we are made for each other
If I am the door and you are the handle
We are made for each other
If I am the house and you are the garden
We are made for each other

When the trees grow and the lakes fill with water
That then means we are regrown
New to this school and this big place, new people
But you and me are one
Standing strong.

Summer Porter-Dodds
The Blyth Academy, Blyth

Worth More

Scuttling along a rock
With a bird's-eye view of the sea
Watching the dark water dance
Current flowing underneath me

Being one of many creatures
That call this vast space home
A place of endless wonders
Where I could always roam

So precious, it needs protecting
From human beings' hands
Plagued by ignorance and carelessness
Of litter from their lands

Every day, I see the impact
Of rubbish left behind
I wonder if that was their home
Would they even mind?

It doesn't just disappear
Because it's thrown away
The wrapper of a crisp packet
Can last almost 30,000 days

I see the damage done
To our home down deep below
A fish can be entangled
In a litter that is thrown

Some creatures don't survive
Some of my family and my friends
A crab like me is helpless
And will lead to an unfortunate end

Human litter in our waters
Free to flow from shore to shore
We need people to be considerate
And remember, this is our home

So humans, all I ask
Is to consider generations to come
Do you want us to be around
Or for us to all be gone?

Do you want us to exist
Or to be part of the past?
If so, protect our aquatic home
By disposing of your trash

No flyaway excuses
Or no bin there to be used
Place it in your pocket
Littering doesn't make you cool

We share one world between us
All creatures of this Earth

No excuses, no mistakes
Please do what it takes

Protect the seas for all their worth.

Ellie Scantlebury (13)
The Blyth Academy, Blyth

Please Think Twice

Turtles near the house on their back
Live wherever, away from the track
With big wide eyes and four padded feet
Able to see right down the street.

But something up there along the shore
Caught his eye, then there was more
Paper, bottles, nets and a bag
Now is the time for us to nag.

On the shore, we struggle to find
A safe way down to bathe and unwind
So when you go for a day at the beach
Take rubbish home or be as guilty as a leech.

Just think about how the turtles feel
When they can't get home to talk to the seals
Both love to swim, show off and play
So please listen to what the turtle has to say.

Just think twice as this is my home
While you walk here to mindfully roam.

Callie Dickinson (12)
The Blyth Academy, Blyth

Failure Girl

Look at that, I made a mistake again
How many times does this make?
See, these scars keep opening up
Despite how I try to close them
Look at that, they say ignorance is bliss
Oh, how good I've gotten at this
See, they say anything they want about me
No one wants me

My wounds laid bare
It hurts, really hurts
I need to act tough
It hurts, really hurts
I can't breathe
It hurts, really hurts

Failure they say
No matter what I do or how hard I try
It's no use
I just want to be loved, I want love
I have to fake my way through
Would it work if I tried to smile
Just a little bit more?

Look at that, my skin is scraped again
How many times does this make?
See, my traumas keep oozing out
Despite how I try to hide them

Look at that, I've held it in and made it seem like it's okay
Oh, how good I've gotten at this
See, they say anything about me
I'm showered in their disdain and covered in bruises

This feeling
Is making me quiver
This inferiority complex
Is making me quiver
I can't breathe
I'm completely empty inside

Would it work if I tried to keep a more natural smile?

If I could be reborn
I hope to be a girl who is loved
Once I've cried my eyes out
I'm sure, very sure
I'll be able to smile tomorrow
Won't I?

Goodbye
To my life full of failures...

Aisha Anwar (14)
The Blyth Academy, Blyth

Stuck

I'm stuck,
Living my life, hoping for luck.
Look what you could have done,
Look what you could become,
Thousands of sufferers from this curse,
But still, you poison the universe.
So much I want to say,
So little I can do, lay
On this bed, in this room,
The darkness really begins to loom
On my despair, on my hope, on my life,
All my friends begin to sacrifice
All their dreams, all their lies
Do you really think we want to say our goodbyes?
As the heat rises and sets,
All you do is place your bets,
The money, the people cry,
As their hopes begin to die.
Who cares what we make?
Who cares if it's safe?
If we see the Earth in a brighter light?
What can we do?
The world is changing so much.
But still, I can do nothing.
A life, a curse.

So many things I want to do, want to say,
But still, you do nothing.
The world is breaking down all the time,
But what can I do when I'm stuck here?
Who wants to hear my views?
This person I have become, this life I have to live,
But what do you do?
Nothing.
Thousands of people are suffering, dying,
But we still care, we still count
The heat, the rush…

Amy Ruth Kennedy (11)
The Blyth Academy, Blyth

The World

What you become is you,
But while you drive around
With Starbucks, you kill fellow
Friends and burn me.

There are no superheroes,
But we need heroes, people
Who believe happiness will come
Be the changes they want.

Burning and killing won't help
I fight back, you depend on them
Your own children to save you!

Stop! Stop! Stop!
It's you scaring me.
It's you melting me.
It's you leaving them to suffer in your mess.

You burn me
I will burn you
You kill me
I kill you
You scar me, I scar you
Don't forget, I have power too.

You don't have much time
Before we become no more,
Start caring and loving this world more!

Holly Wight (11)
The Blyth Academy, Blyth

We Can Change!

2119, born in a hospital in York,
My great-grandparents used to live in Blyth,
But now, there is no such place.

2119, barely one week old, black smoke flying in the air,
People coughing and unwell,
It is their fault they are suffering.

2120, one-year-old, all the fossil fuels,
Nearly half the Earth's population wiped out,
Nearly half the towns and countries gone.

2122, three years old now,
I am a baby,
But have seen years of pain and suffering.

2122, three-quarters of our soul,
Of us,
Gone.

2133, dead,
Because of you,
We have teamed up to destroy Earth.

We can still change this,
So stop and do something
Before it is too late!

Eve Rowe (11)
The Blyth Academy, Blyth

Acceptance

Do stories always end with happy endings?
What's the point in being the same as the person next to me?
We have to find our voice
We can't copy off someone else's work, their actions
I don't want fame or money
I want love, acceptance

I won't ask for acceptance and to be accepted anymore
But I ask to be treated like a person and not a thing
I'm a person underneath this shell I call a body that protects me from words so
We deserve human rights and to be acknowledged for who we are
And not for who you want us to be

This is acceptance, it makes the world go round
It's your turn to change the world
Enjoy life.

Iona Thomas (11)
The Blyth Academy, Blyth

We All Have Rights

I'm Rosa Parks
And what you're about to hear
Is how I showed that we all have rights
You won't believe your ears

I was sat on the bus
A white male come onto the bus
He told me to move so he could sit there
I said no
He couldn't believe his ears

I got escorted off the bus
Into a police car
Found out I was in jail
For a couple of days
I couldn't believe my ears

Every black male and female
Still didn't know
They had power
I couldn't believe my eyes

I heard
Martin Luther King
Announce that black people
Have rights
I couldn't believe my eyes.

Dyllan Jon Corrie (13)
The Blyth Academy, Blyth

Mr Human

I wake up,
Breathing still heavy,
The thunderous clap echoed.
I open my eyes.

Tears welled up in my eyes,
These monstrous sounds
Were mankind. I frowned
And poured with salty water.

Look there, a human,
Stealing his horn.
Look here, a gun aimed at his head,
Look now, a pack divided.

All the cost of the use of us,
Our horns make decorations
For the cost of our lives.

Please, Mr Human,
Leave us alone.
We only wanted to live at home,
Now my family is dead,
All because you needed a quilt for your bed.
I hope you have a heavy head,
Look now, all the rhinos are dead.

Ben Yarwood (12)
The Blyth Academy, Blyth

Resurface

Bathed in sleet
My eyes grow weak
Palms pressed to the ice
I strike and punch

A fire erupts in my chest
A shrieking, howling inferno
I yearn for oxygen
I yearn for life

Gravity is pulling at my legs
I feel its claws wrap around my ankle like a sea monster's
Eventually, I'm dragged down
Sinking

As my eyes burn
And my hands numb
I feel your arms surround me

You lift me up into the sunlight
Onto land where the birds are singing
The plane where happiness is enduring

My heart flutters against yours
Beating a jig of life against my ribs.

Hannah Marshall (14)
The Blyth Academy, Blyth

The Light

I can't believe my eyes,
How come most of the trees died?
This isn't fair.
This is something I can't bare,
Look at what we've done,
Look at what the world has become,
I can't stand this heat,
Look at the plastic under my feet.
Why?
Why would you do this?
You said you would fix it,
All I see are your lies
And the animals begin to cry,
Their homes you let melt away,
So that you get your money through the day.
But don't worry at night,
I have no fear to fight,
All I have is a sacrifice,
So once again, this world can see the light.

Cassidy Dunn (12)
The Blyth Academy, Blyth

Teens

All is different
All is weird
Nothing is right
From lesson, to lesson
To life, to life
Desire changes
Challenge your life

Trying to fit in
The best that you can
Hanging out
With the popular gang

Your appearance can change
From day to day
Surviving to fit in
Just right
Struggling with peers
Hiding your fears

All is not what it seems
I close my eyes
There are different dreams
I feel happy and sad
Angry and mad
Becoming a teenager can make you sad!

Jean Carr (12)
The Blyth Academy, Blyth

Shadows

All they do is stand and stare
While I am alone over here
Alone I am and will always be

There is no hope in my life
There is nothing left for me

This shadow in my mind never stops
As it feeds off my pain
It will never leave

Negativity is all I own
The positivity was stolen long ago

Home is no different
Alone I am and will always be

My room is a mirror
It reflects the pain
I never forget
It's always there

The pain
The torture
The fear...

Phillipa Eve Turner (13)
The Blyth Academy, Blyth

Bullies

Bullies are not nice,
They stink like rice,
They think they are hard,
But they are really not,
They act like they are,
But being cool is being nice.

They don't realise how hurtful the words are,
They shouldn't be doing this to other people,
They think it is fun,
But it is really hurtful to other people
And people are miserable,
They should think about what they are doing
And they should think about what they are saying,
They should be nice from now on.

Bethany Welsh (11)
The Blyth Academy, Blyth

Poor Baby Seal

Poor baby seal,
Oh, how do you feel?
Watching her there,
Them skinning her hair.
Your little paws flipping fast,
Trying not to see the past.
Your mother's squeals,
Oh, how do you feel?

Your perplexed face,
Oh, why in this place?
Your nerves are high,
Reaching the sky,
The clouds reminding you of her,
That soft, fluffy, white fur
That they stole from her.

Poor baby seal,
Oh, how do you feel?

Caitlin Humble (12)
The Blyth Academy, Blyth

Jesy Nelson - Little Mix

No matter what, always stick with
The people you love the most
You will realise it's better than being alone
But remember, always believe in yourself
No matter what happens
Do not let anyone bring you down
Because you are perfect the way you are
And there will always be one you
Don't let anyone tell you anything else
Because they aren't worth your time.

Ella Woods (12)
The Blyth Academy, Blyth

Why Do You Do This?

Why do you do this?
Is there something we haven't done?
If we were gone,
Would you want to be alone?

And, before I die,
I end up in space,
At least you're still on the ground,
Guess I've won the race.

As God looks down upon you,
You do not appear;
But if he saw you,
He'd snap you like the antler from a reindeer.

James Oram (11)
The Blyth Academy, Blyth

Here In Space

Here, up in space,
I see the Earth's face,
Watching it sink and sink,
There is a lot of pollution,
Soon there will be no solution,
Here, up in space.

Here, up in space,
I see the Earth's face,
Green and pristine,
Slowly decaying and withering away
And the white ice,
Boiling away like rice,
Here, up in space.

Alfie Finley McPhee (11)
The Blyth Academy, Blyth

Besties

You've got my back, I've got yours
I'll help you out anytime
To see you cry, to see you hurt
Makes me weep and want to die
And, if you agree to never fight
It wouldn't matter who is wrong or right
If a broken or shattered heart needs to be mended
I'll be right there till the very end
Because we are besties until the end.

Brooke Porter-Dodds (11)
The Blyth Academy, Blyth

Bullying

B ullying is bad for the community
U seless and uncalled for
L oud and unsettled
L ikeable is all I want to be
Y ou can stay strong
I ntense and unwanted
N ot a good thing to go through
G o to get help if it happens to someone.

Skye George
The Blyth Academy, Blyth

Don't Judge

Be yourself
Love who you are
And love who you want
It doesn't matter who you are
And what you want to do
Don't judge who people are
Put yourself in the position
Of that person and people
Discriminating others
Don't judge.

Kieran Hemsley (11)
The Blyth Academy, Blyth

Choices

May your choices affect one person
But one word can change the world
Love or hate, I'm your mate
There are no heroes in life
Just monsters
Being classy is just peer pressure
Once you click send, you can't unsend.

Holly Ann Morgan (12)
The Blyth Academy, Blyth

Mammy

I open my eyes, all that I see
These giant people staring at me

Where is my mammy?
Where can she be?

I wish my mammy was next to me
I see my mammy coming over from the tree
So happy now, I'll be.

Katelin Jane Bell (11)
The Blyth Academy, Blyth

My New School

N ew friends
E xcited
W riting new words

S cary
C hange
H appy
O verwhelmed
O bjectives
L earning.

Ayah Ghaham (12)
The Blyth Academy, Blyth

YOUNG WRITERS INFORMATION

We hope you have enjoyed reading this book – and that you will continue to in the coming years.

If you're a young writer who enjoys reading and creative writing, or the parent of an enthusiastic poet or story writer, do visit our website **www.youngwriters.co.uk**. Here you will find free competitions, workshops and games, as well as recommended reads, a poetry glossary and our blog. There's lots to keep budding writers motivated to write!

If you would like to order further copies of this book, or any of our other titles, then please give us a call or order via your online account.

Young Writers
Remus House
Coltsfoot Drive
Peterborough
PE2 9BF
(01733) 890066
info@youngwriters.co.uk

Join in the conversation!
Tips, news, giveaways and much more!

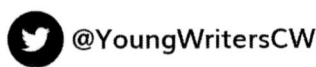